W9-BZU-459

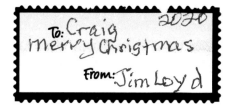

To: Craig
merry Christmas
From: Jim Loyd
2020

One-Minute
PRAYERS®
FOR
HUNTERS

STEVE CHAPMAN

HARVEST HOUSE PUBLISHERS
EUGENE, OREGON

Cover by Bryce Williamson

Cover Images © Surovtseva, Lava4images, Jessicahyde, Aleksandarvelasevic, DamianKuzdak / iStock

ONE-MINUTE PRAYERS is a registered trademark of The Hawkins Children's LLC. Harvest House Publishers, Inc., is the exclusive licensee of the federally registered trademark ONE-MINUTE PRAYERS.

ONE-MINUTE PRAYERS® FOR HUNTERS
Copyright © 2017 by Steve Chapman
Published by Harvest House Publishers
Eugene, Oregon 97402
www.harvesthousepublishers.com

ISBN 978-0-7369-6707-5 (hardcover)
ISBN 978-0-7369-6708-2 (eBook)

This book is dedicated to my late father,
Paul J. Chapman,
and my mother,
Lillian,
who diligently taught me the value of prayer.

Stirred Up!

I am stirring up your sincere mind.

2 PETER 3:1

Lord, just as outdoor writers can stir anticipation in me about a new, upcoming hunting season, You know how to get my spiritual juices flowing. You do it through the writers of Your recorded Word, and I thank You for it. Help me understand and never forget the precepts for right living that are found in the Bible. You are a kind Father for loving me enough to inspire my heart. Your timing is always perfect, especially when I need a special boost of faith. I offer my thanks to You in Your Son's holy and exciting name. Amen.

Hearing the Call

I called you but you did not answer.

JEREMIAH 7:13

Father in heaven, as one who was once so dangerously lost in the deep woods of sin, I offer my sincere thanks to You for calling out to me. Your voice of hope that I heard through Your bold yet compassionate earthly messenger is the sweetest sound I've ever heard. Words can't express how glad I am that I didn't ignore Your call. They can never adequately describe the joy of being rescued by Your mercy and grace from eternal separation from You. Your loving hands of grace have set me on the path of peace. I never want to be guilty of not answering when You talk to me. I trust that for the rest of my days You will speak to my heart when You see me wandering off the trail of truth. I pray in Christ's name. Amen.

Carry Them Back

Rejoice with me, for I have found
my sheep which was lost!

LUKE 15:6

Carry Them Back

Oh, sweet Shepherd, hear me today
Someone I love has wandered away
If anyone can find them, dear Lord, I know it's You
This is my request
O Father, when you do

Carry them back to Your field of forgiveness
Carry them back to Your pastures of grace
Safe on your shoulders cradle them gently
Carry them back, back home I pray

Oh, dear Jesus, how well I recall
When I was that one You carried back home
That's why I'll keep praying
As You search those dark hills
For the one I miss so much
I believe You will…carry them back[1]

No Other Name

*There is salvation in no one else; for there is
no other name under heaven
that has been given among men
by which we must be saved.*

ACTS 4:12

Jesus, I pray that You will enlighten the eyes of my heart so that I will know what is the hope of Your calling, what are the riches of the glory of Your inheritance in the saints, and what is the surpassing greatness of Your power toward all who believe. According to Your Word, these blessings are in accordance with the working of the strength of Your might, which God the Father brought about in You, His Son, when He raised You from the dead and seated You at His right hand in the heavenly places, far above all rule and authority and power and dominion, and above every name that is named, not only in this age but also in the one to come. The vastness of the sky above me only hints at how great Your name is. There's no other name through which I can be saved. Worthy are You to be praised for You have done great things! Amen.

Trusting God in All Things

We know that God causes all things to work
together for good to those who love God.

ROMANS 8:28

Dear God, in those times when things have turned out much better for me than I expected, I know it was You who made things work together for my good. You've proven that You can and will do this for those who love You. I think of young David, who faced the Philistine giant on behalf of You and Your people with a homemade sling. He drew on his consistent practice, his previous experience, and most important, his youthful and zealous love for You as His God. And the outcome was victory. With this encouraging story in mind, my love for You compels me to submit all that I am and all that I have to You. Please use whatever is needed to bring about Your will for my life. In Christ's name I pray. Amen.

Keeping a Listening Ear

The Lord Himself will descend from heaven with a shout, with the voice of the archangel and with the trumpet of God, and the dead in Christ will rise first. Then we who are alive and remain will be caught up together with them in the clouds to meet the Lord in the air.

1 Thessalonians 4:16-17

Dear God, as a hunter I know the disappointment that comes with missing an opportunity for success because I failed to hear a sound that tells me an animal is nearby. Though I feel defeated, regret can never compare to the despair I'd feel if I failed for any reason to hear the voice of the archangel and the trumpet that will announce Your return. Help me to live in Your grace so that the ears of my heart will experience the joy of that amazing sound. In Christ's mighty name I pray. Amen.

He Will Answer

Call to Me and I will answer you, and
I will tell you great and
mighty things, which you do not know.

JEREMIAH 33:3

Father in heaven, as a hunter I know the thrill of watching a turkey, a duck, a deer, an elk, and other animals respond when I use my man-made calls. The fact that I can communicate somewhat with creatures so vastly different from me is amazing. But far more incredible than that is the realization that You, the God and awesome Maker of this universe, hear me when I call to You. What love and compassion You show by being willing to hear someone so frail in spirit and weak in the flesh.

I offer my deepest thanks for opening Your ear to me. I can never adequately express how comforting it is to know I can call on You anytime. Blessed be Your holy name. In Christ I say amen.

Obedience

You may eat freely.

GENESIS 2:16

God, when I read in Genesis that You said to Adam and Eve, "You may eat freely," I realize You're not just being a kind and wonderful Father. You are also being loving enough to give me guidelines that are good for me. I'm grateful for all the things I can partake of in this life without worrying that You might be displeased by them. On the other hand, I want to know what You want me to avoid. Just like I want to avoid the trouble that can come with ignoring a "No Hunting" sign or a "No Trespassing" sign, I want to obey You. I definitely don't want the spiritual death that comes with disobedience. For the sake of pleasing You, I ask for Your guidance…and Your grace to follow it. In Christ's holy and perfect name, amen.

Harmony in Camp

*Behold, how good and how pleasant it is
for brothers to dwell together in unity!*

PSALM 133:1

Lord, it's amazing how harmonious a group of men can be at a deer camp. No doubt it's because we all arrive with the same passion and purpose—the hunt. Our shared interest leads to conversation that's enjoyable, a great willingness to be helpful to one another, and best of all, a peacefulness while we're together. How great it would be if that kind of oneness of thought could be found in every place where Your people gather. How pleased You would surely be to see Your followers congregate, with each person offering a friendly smile and a readiness to share in the joy of Your love, grace, redemption, and provision. I pray that You will forgive us for those times when our division fails to please You. Help us strive for the goal of dwelling together in unity and peace. We want this for Your glory. In Jesus' name, amen.

Food for the Soul

I encourage you to take some food,
for this is for your preservation.

ACTS 27:34

Father in heaven, You know well that the hunt can sometimes be so mind and energy consuming that a hunter can forget to take in sustenance in the form of food and water. Then the problem that arises from ignoring the appetite is that we grow weak and risk losing our focus. The result can be anything from the simple mistake of making a poor shot to becoming faint and falling out of a tree stand, from getting lost to injuring someone else.

I know similar hazards exist on a spiritual level too. As Your follower, it's not good when I don't nourish myself with Your Word, spend time in fellowship with other believers, and regularly meet with You in prayer. Help me recognize and cultivate a hunger for You. I want to partake of Your presence because I know I need Your strength for the journey. In Christ's name, amen.

Not Yet

You will hear of wars and rumors of wars.
See that you are not troubled;
for all these things must come to
pass, but the end is not yet.

MATTHEW 24:6 NKJV

Lord, I'm familiar with the words "not yet." I've used them at times to calm my nerves when a sizable deer is just out of range but approaching. Coaxing myself to wait patiently has worked more than once to help close the deal.

In the same way, "not yet" is my cue to realize trouble and distress will be here on earth until You put a stop to it. I need to wait patiently, but that's not easy to do. You're very aware that sometimes I wonder if the cares of this life and the suffering it brings will ever end. In those times, it's hard to trust that You will come as promised and deliver me from trouble. When I question if that day will come, help me remember that You've already provided the encouragement and comfort I need when You said the end is "not yet." Even so, come quickly, Lord Jesus. Amen.

On the Right Side

He who is not with Me is against Me;
and he who does not gather
with Me scatters.

MATTHEW 12:30

L ord, I thank You for Your grace that drew me into a relationship with You. It is a blessing beyond measure to be on Your side. I know with You I'm safe and my soul can rest. I trust You to show me any place in my heart that isn't fully devoted to You. Help me turn it over to You. May this continue until all that will not praise You in my heart is totally undone. In the sweet name of Jesus I pray. Amen.

Usefulness

You are old and advanced in years, and very much of the land remains to be possessed.

JOSHUA 13:1

Lord, I'm always inspired when I meet and talk to elderly hunters who still deeply enjoy going into Your great outdoors. To see the excitement in their eyes when they talk about trophies to pursue, hills to climb, and woods to explore is inspiring. I want to be just as excited and energized always—but not just about hunting. I want to serve You with enthusiasm all the days of my life. There are more victories to experience, more souls who need to hear the good news of the redemption You offer, and new trails of spiritual adventures to walk.

Please continue to reveal Your purpose for me in every season of my life. I want to do whatever You desire for me to do. Thank You for the opportunity to serve You. May others see Your grace as I gladly perform the tasks You set before me. In Christ's name I pray. Amen.

Good Advice

*Jesus said, "Are you still lacking
in understanding also?"*

MATTHEW 15:16

God, just like those times when I've asked for advice from an experienced hunter and gotten the insights I needed, I come to You for wisdom. Too many times in the past I needed direction in my life but failed to ask You for it. Instead, I leaned on my own understanding. Every time I've made that mistake, the outcome was never good. I humbly admit my need for Your light. Give me the patience to wait for You to give it. I want to walk on the path You set before me. In the bright, shining name of Jesus I pray. Amen.

The Hurting

*The LORD is near to the brokenhearted
and saves those who are crushed in spirit.*

PSALM 34:18

Father in heaven, as I enjoy the quiet and calm of the outdoors, I know there are those who are in the midst of terrible chaos right now. Their hearts have been broken, and their spirits have been crushed. I know of abandoned children who need the comfort of Your presence. I'm aware of those who have been wounded in their hearts by family members, friends, or even total strangers. I think of those whose souls are bearing the heavy weight of life-threatening health issues. I think of ones who long to have children but have empty arms because of infertility.

Lord, the needs are endless and the depth of despair in people is beyond measure. You are aware of *every* individual's needs. Be near each one at this moment. Bless each person with an undeniable sense of Your love and care. I pray this in the compassionate name of Christ Jesus. Amen.

A Practical Life

*Just as they did not see fit to acknowledge
God any longer, God gave them
over to a depraved mind, to do those
things which are not proper.*

ROMANS 1:28

Dear God, I pray for the courage to avoid doing those things that are corrupt, perverted, or improper in Your eyes. I don't want to do anything illegal, including hunting without a license or out of season, that would make me want to lie or cheat or in any way dishonor You. There's nothing practical or worthwhile about sin.

I want my mind and heart to be committed to knowing You and to living the way You've asked me to live. This is my desire simply because it's a spiritually sensible, energy-conserving, anxiety-free path to experiencing Your peace. Please show me how to avoid doing things that cost me strength and don't glorify You. Blessed be Your name for the help You give. In Christ's name I pray. Amen.

Fresh Breath

Let your speech always be with grace.

COLOSSIANS 4:6

God, I've often been detected by the incredibly sensitive nose of a deer. As a friend told me, "If you're breathing, you're busted." My human odor is carried on my breath and easily discerned by alert animals. It's as though they're offended by it. That's why I chew on apples when in a tree stand.

When it comes to my life as one of Your followers, God, I want to have fresh breath when I speak so I honor You and lift You up to those around me. How thankful I am for Your written Word that I can chew on to freshen my speech so people will know I love You. Help me be sound in speech and offer people the blessings of Your grace. I ask You to help me do this daily in the name of Your sweet Son, Jesus. Amen.

Built-In Blessing

Blessed be the God and Father of our
Lord Jesus Christ, who has blessed
us with every spiritual blessing in
the heavenly places in Christ.

EPHESIANS 1:3

Father in heaven, when I see animals that have massive antlers, such as deer, elk, and caribou, I think of the genes they inherited when they were born. Everything they needed to grow their trophy racks was in them from day one, and everything they eat as they mature adds to the growth.

In a similar way, everything I need to reflect You and bear witness for You was given to me on the day I came to You in repentance and began living for You. You placed grace, truth, strength, hope, and many other components into my life so I can bear fruit for You. And what a spiritual blessing they are! Help me rest in the knowledge that as You feed me with the nutrients that come from the rich soil of Your Word, I become a fruit bearer for Your glory. In the name of Jesus, amen.

Out of My Comfort Zone

*Peter got out of the boat, and walked
on the water and came toward Jesus.*

MATTHEW 14:29

Lord Jesus, like Your servant Peter, who was brave enough to step out of the safety and comfort of the boat and walk toward You, I want to be willing to walk outside my comfort zone to tell others about You. Forgive me for those times I've yielded to fear and not seized an opportunity to speak about You. Help me from this day on to step out for You in faith and share Your love. In Your name I pray. Amen.

At This Moment

Day and night they do not cease to
say, "HOLY, HOLY, HOLY, is THE LORD
GOD, THE ALMIGHTY, WHO WAS AND
WHO IS AND WHO IS TO COME."

REVELATION 4:8

Lord, when I can't be in the woods or in the fields hunting, I often imagine what's going on out there. During turkey season, I just know there are big gobblers strutting in my favorite field while I'm at work. During deer season, I can see in my mind's eye a nice, edible doe passing right under my tree stand I'm not in.

This reminds me of what is going on in heaven while I'm not there. Your written Word tells me there is constant worship in Your presence, and You are receiving the praise You deserve. Almighty God of Abraham, Isaac, and Jacob, Maker of this universe, right now I join the hosts of heaven who are singing praises to You. You alone are worthy of worship and adoration. I give You thanks for Your lovingkindness toward me. Blessed be Your holy name forever and ever. In the name of Jesus, Your eternal Son, I add my amen and amen!

Life on the Alert

Be of sober spirit, be on the alert. Your adversary, the devil, prowls around like a roaring lion, seeking someone to devour.

1 PETER 5:8

God, I enjoy watching the cautious behavior of the animals You created. What a privilege to see the way a deer raises its head and checks the wind for an unusual odor or to see how a turkey uses its amazingly keen eyesight to watch for the slightest movement. Your creatures inspire me to be more aware of the dangers around me. Help me keep my mind to the wind to detect any false doctrines that might try to lead me astray. Help me train my ears to know a lie when it's told. Open my eyes to spiritual pitfalls I must avoid. I ask for Your help because I don't want to fall victim to the devil, whose mission is to destroy and devour souls like mine. Blessed be Your holy name, God, for leading me to the truth. Amen.

Invited

I did not come to call the
righteous, but sinners.

MARK 2:17

Almighty God, being invited to hunt on a very exclusive and productive piece of property is exciting for any hunter. But Lord, how greatly that privilege pales in comparison to Your invitation to come into Your presence. To think that You, the Maker and God of this entire universe and beyond, long for a sinner like me to be near You is a blessing that can't be measured or understood. To have been drawn to You through Jesus and the Holy Spirit is, without exception, the most important thing that has ever happened to me. You are indeed a wonderful and loving God. Your kindness compels me to live daily in a way that will honor the love and acceptance You've shown me. In Your Son's holy name I pray. Amen.

Drop the Stone of Judgment

He who is without sin among you, let
him be the first to throw a stone at her.

JOHN 8:7

O merciful Father, through the account of the woman who was caught in the act of adultery and was about to be unmercifully stoned, You have supplied a great insight for me. Those men were just a stone's throw away from committing an evil act that would have destroyed them as well as the accused woman. How kind of You to help them see the error of their thinking by challenging their sense of right and wrong. I ask that You do the same for me. If You see a stone of judgment in my hand, help me face my own sinfulness and offer mercy to people who need Your mercy and grace as well. And just as those men dropped their death stones and walked away from a potentially bad choice, help me do the same. I want to do this for Your glory alone. In Christ's name I ask for Your help and guidance. Amen.

Eat and Share

He said to me, "Son of man, eat
what you find; eat this scroll, and
go, speak to the house of Israel."

Ezekiel 3:1

God, thank You for feeding my soul with the scroll of Your Word. I know it will prepare me well if I'm to speak on Your behalf. Approaching people about their need for You can be as risky today as it was in Ezekiel's day, but I don't want to fail to follow Your urging to do it. I confess that the possibility of being called hate-filled, intolerant, nosy, or an extremist is troubling.

When I feel hesitant to stand up for You, give me the courage to speak boldly because of the authority of Your written Word that I've consumed. Help me to speak for You with an attitude of humility that comes from personally experiencing Your tender grace and mercy. As an act of kindness, I want to warn those whose errors will destroy them so they can turn to You to save their souls from everlasting death and separation from You.

I pray this in the mighty name of Your loving Son, Jesus. Amen.

Sowing Seeds of Honor

Honor your father and your mother.

Exodus 20:12

Father in heaven, when I hunt around a cornfield, I'm reminded that whatever we sow, we will reap. When it comes to my children, I know that the only way to reap the harvest of being honored by them is to sow the seeds of kindness in their hearts. Help me do just that. I thank You in advance for any benefit I may glean in my later years by treating them in godly ways as they are growing up. Ultimately, may You be honored most of all by the outcome. In Christ's name I pray. Amen.

Remember Me

Jesus, remember me when You
come in Your kingdom!

LUKE 23:42

Lord Jesus, what great mercy You showed to the thief on the cross next to You. I need that mercy too.

Remember Me

O Lord, I know I'm not worthy
To receive Your mercy, yet You look at me
With eyes full of love and pity.
Please forgive me as You have done
For those who watch us die
I need Your mercy, hear my cry

Lord, will You remember
Will You remember
When life is over…remember me
There's nothing I can offer for Your favor
Still I ask You

When You come into Your kingdom
Remember me

Oh, I am lost, I know it's true
But my hope is now in you[2]

Heads Up

*There will be signs in the sun, moon and
stars... When these things begin to take
place, stand up and lift up your heads,
because your redemption is drawing near.*

LUKE 21:25,28 NIV

God, sometimes I've missed a chance at sighting an animal because I was looking down at my cell phone. As a result of the distraction, I didn't see or hear the movement that might have alerted me that a trophy was near. This modern-era mistake can produce some well-deserved self-kicking, but I know my disappointment would be far worse if I missed the signs of Your coming. I don't want to be so immersed in high-tech conversations and entertainment that I become spiritually slumped over and unable to lift my head as You tell me to do. Help me look up so I will see Your glorious appearance in the heavens. I pray this for myself, for my loved ones, and for my friends. Help us all look up to see You. In the name of the coming Lord Jesus Christ I pray. Amen.

Dependability

I have no one else like him.

PHILIPPIANS 2:20 NIV

By grace You have not only redeemed me, Lord, but You have also entrusted me with sharing with others the hope found in the good news of the salvation You offer. I want to be a faithful messenger...a dependable servant. When all is said and done, I hope it will be said of me what Paul said about Timothy: "I have no one else like him." May it be so in Your precious and holy name. Amen.

Not Surprised

Fellow Israelites, why does this surprise you?

ACTS 3:12 NIV

Blessed God and Creator, if I were to say I'm surprised that You were able to build this incredible planet and all its neighbors in the universe, I would imply that I doubted You could have done it. Instead of saying, "I'm surprised," I simply say, "I'm amazed." And when I hear that You've healed someone, or miraculously met someone's desperate need, or torn down a stronghold of the devil, I declare, "I'm amazed, but I'm not surprised!" Why? Because my God can do anything. You are indeed *amazing*, God. And may my saying so never surprise You. Amen.

Believing Is Seeing

*Jesus said to him, "Because you have
seen Me, have you believed? Blessed are
they who did not see, and yet believed."*

Lord Jesus, when it comes to believing You are real, I want to be as trusting as the young, inexperienced hunter who was sitting with a veteran deer hunter. The seasoned teacher said, "There's a nice buck standing over there just inside the woods." The young hunter looked hard for half a minute without seeing it. Trusting his teacher, he said, "I don't see it yet, but I believe it's there."

With that picture in mind, Lord, I offer my deepest thanks to You for sending Your Holy Spirit to speak to my heart about Your majesty and grace, as well as the eternal salvation You provide through Your sacrifice on the cross. I have yet to see You with my eyes, but I believe You are who You say You are. Blessed be Your holy name! In Your excellent name I pray. Amen.

Clear the Field

*Get rid of all moral filth and the evil that
is so prevalent and humbly accept the
word planted in you, which can save you.*

JAMES 1:21 NIV

Father in heaven, in the way that a new field needs to be cleared of rocks, stumps, and anything else that would hinder the planting of seed, I want to rid the field of my heart of sin. I desire this so that the everlasting seed of Your truth can be sown in me. Help me identify the things that do not please You. Grant me courage to do what is necessary to remove them. And that which I can't get rid of, I trust You to complete the cleansing.

Forgive me for letting sin damage me far too long. I need Your grace to be cleansed and to share Your love with others. In Christ's name, amen.

I Will

On the glorious splendor of Your majesty
and on Your wonderful
works, I will meditate.

PSALM 145:5

O God, our great and awesome Creator, I understand the value of meditating on Your goodness, on Your majesty, on Your wonderful works. Thinking about You always leads me to worship You. I know it pleases You when I do. I confess that I don't always *want to* engage in meditation because the cares of life consume my thoughts. In those times, I need to *will myself to* worship You. Being in Your great outdoors effectively turns my lack of *want to* into a full-blown *will to* worship You with all my heart. What a wonderful place to be to see Your greatness and meditate on Your majesty. I trust that when I set my will to go outdoors to enjoy Your presence, You will meet me there. In Christ's name, amen.

Wait for It!

*Do not be afraid, Daniel, for from
the first day that you set your heart on
understanding this and on humbling
yourself before your God, your words were
heard, and I have come in response.*

DANIEL 10:12

Dear God, You know there are times when I wonder if You hear my prayers. And You also know very well how I struggle to keep trusting when I'm unsure. Forgive me for the doubts I've entertained while waiting for an answer from You. Thank You for the encouragement found in what You said to Daniel after he prayed. Knowing that You heard him the first time he humbly prayed helps me feel hopeful that my sincere cries reach Your ear when I first call out. As for Your response…I will wait for it. Amen.

The Tragedy of Deceit

*In later times some will fall away from
the faith, paying attention to deceitful
spirits and doctrines of demons.*

1 Timothy 4:1

Father in heaven, most of us who hunt deer have heard a sound we thought was made by a big, approaching buck only to learn we were fooled by a scratching turkey, a fat possum lumbering through the woods, or even a stray dog trotting by. When that happens, our excitement bubble is instantly deflated.

Thank You for warning me to be careful about the dangers of listening to and following after deceitful spirits and teachings promoted by demons. I'm aware that if I believe a lie and end up falling away from my fellowship with You, it's a spiritual tragedy. Please give me Your guidance to help me recognize an untruth and to not give it even a moment of my attention. Show me how to train my ear to know Your truth when I hear it. May it be so to Your glory. In Your Son's name I pray. Amen.

God's Word Doesn't Miss

*As the rain and the snow come down from
heaven…so will My word be which goes
forth from My mouth; it will not return
to Me empty, without accomplishing
what I desire, and without succeeding
in the matter for which I sent it.*

Isaiah 55:10-11

O God, how grateful I am that when You send
forth the words of Your mouth, they connect
precisely with the mark at which You aim. When my
heart is Your target, and I am blessed with the life-
altering truths You help me understand, my spirit
soars with life like a carefree dove in flight. I praise
You for Your limitless skill with Your words. In the
name of Your Word made flesh, Jesus Christ, I pray.
Amen.

An Understanding Smile

A cheerful look brings joy to the heart.

Proverbs 15:30 nlt

Lord, I've hunted with friends and seen the sadness and disappointment on their faces when they've wounded an animal and were unable to recover it. The raw emotions are obvious. I've found that the best medicine for their aching soul is a smile. I know it's true because I've been soothed by an understanding, upbeat look. It's in those times that I'm especially thankful that You gave mankind the ability to smile. It's amazing how uplifting an optimistic expression can be. It's certainly been a blessing to me.

I pray for Your help to recognize when others are in need of my smile. May it be so not only in the woods but anywhere in life that I'm with people. In Christ's name, amen.

Imitators

*Be imitators of me, just as
I also am of Christ.*

1 CORINTHIANS 11:1

Father in heaven, it's a huge responsibility to take a young hunter into the woods. Every move I make will leave a lasting impression and forever shape his or her attitude about hunting. In the same way, when it comes to influencing Your less experienced followers, I know I have an important role to play. I appreciate any opportunity You give me to be an example of Your grace, but I know I'd be foolish to ever say, "Be an imitator of me" without adding, "as I imitate Jesus Christ." God, without Your influence on my behavior, I would lead others away from You, not to You.

Help me always act as You would so I'll be worthy to be imitated as Your representative. It's to Your glory I pray. Amen.

Above the Danger

The name of the LORD is a strong tower;
the righteous runs into it and is safe.

PROVERBS 18:10

God, whenever I'm in a tree stand looking at the ground below, I'm reminded of the fact that Your name is like a strong tower. What a tremendous blessing to know that when the enemy of my soul is in pursuit of me or those I love, the invitation to run to You is always good. In Your tower I will always be safe from whatever or whoever wants to cause me harm because *You* are there! Thank You that You are willing and able to lift me above the troubles of this life and set my spirit in the shelter of Your presence. It's the only place I will find true peace for my soul. Blessed be Your mighty name that is above all names. Amen.

Possibilities

Come, see a man who told me everything
I ever did. Could this be the Messiah?

JOHN 4:29 NIV

Father, You know there's nothing that can compel me to go hunting more than the possibility that I'll have a challenging encounter with one of Your wily creatures. Just seeing them in their environment is thrilling and keeps me going back into the woods year after year. In a similar way, one of the reasons I pursue You is because of the peace, joy, security, guidance, provision, forgiveness, light, strength, and other wonderful things You offer that benefit my spirit, my soul, and my body. To know they all are available through Your holy Son, Jesus, compels me to pray for the courage to always be willing to get up out of my spiritual slumber and head to where You are. I want what You have to give. In the name of Jesus, I say thanks for all the possibilities You represent. Your Son is the Messiah…my Messiah. Amen.

He Saw the Wind

*Seeing the wind, [Peter] became
frightened, and beginning to sink,
he cried out, "Lord, save me!"*

MATTHEW 14:30

Lord, I find it interesting that the Scripture says
Peter *saw* the wind. Surely what this refers to is
the sight of the water that was being churned by the
gale that had moved in. This reminds me of the fear
that can rise up when I'm sitting high in a deer stand
and a sudden storm blows in. Seeing the wind in
the violent bending of the branches around me has
caused me to quickly "sink" out of the tree and hurry
to the ground. As I've descended, I've been known to
pray as Peter did, "Lord, save me!"

I know well that life outside the woods can turn
stormy too. When it does and I see the troubling
winds of fear, doubt, and worry, I know it's time to
call out to Jesus. So I will—and I'll be grateful for
Your deliverance. In Christ's name, amen.

Be Ready to Talk

Always be prepared to give an answer
to everyone who asks you to give the
reason for the hope that you have.

1 PETER 3:15 NIV

God, You know well that as a hunter I'm always ready to talk about hunting with anyone who asks me about it. If he or she pushes my "on" button, I'll gladly tell why I like to hunt as well as the stories I've experienced along the way. As long as the listener will lend me an ear, I'll fill it. I want to be just as eager and prepared to tell about Your goodness with people who ask me about my relationship with You. Help me notice when You've opened the door for me to testify to how You've changed my life. Give me the words to say when it happens so my enthusiasm for You comes through. May You receive all the glory. In Christ's name, amen.

Let There Be Light

Your light will rise in darkness.

ISAIAH 58:10

God of all light, there's hardly any moment in nature that speaks of Your power more than sunrise. What an incredible blessing as a hunter to be out there in the predawn to watch the tight grip of darkness be easily loosened by the demanding, growing glow of an early morning sun. To know that You alone are able to overcome darkness with light is a reality that inspires me to the very core of my spirit. What a picture of Your ability to bring life out of death. My heart is filled with hope because You can take any gloomy situation I face and use it to demonstrate Your amazing ability to defeat darkness. May You continue to do so throughout my days. In the bright and blessed name of Jesus, I pray. Amen.

Dressed Right

He has clothed me with garments
of salvation, He has wrapped me
with a robe of righteousness.

ISAIAH 61:10

Father God, I'm grateful for whoever came up with the idea of creating clothing with patterns that blend with nature. My camo has outsmarted the skilled eyes of all kinds of wild game. And when a keen-eyed animal stares at me for a few seconds and then relaxes, I know I've been found acceptable in its eyes.

My camo provides a great picture of the robe of righteousness You've provided for me. When I someday stand in Your presence and am clothed in the righteousness of Your Son, I trust You will find me acceptable. I know if I'm dressed in my own righteousness, the sight will not be pleasing to You. I'm thankful for my camo, but I'm far more grateful for the robe made of the righteousness of Jesus. What an incredible gift and awesome reason to rejoice. In Jesus' mighty name I pray. Amen.

Ruling My Spirit

He who is slow to anger is better than
the mighty, and he who rules his
spirit, than he who captures a city.

PROVERBS 16:32

Father in heaven, You know I've had my share of temper tantrums. I'm aware that it's never a pleasing sight for You to see one of Your children lacking control. I seek Your forgiveness for when I've failed to exercise restraint over my temper and for the times when I've refused to be patient.

I don't want to be so weak in these areas of my life that my actions cause harm to anyone, especially those I deeply love. I don't want to bring reproach on Your name by failing to corral the potentially hurtful anger I might feel. May victory be mine through the strength that *You* alone can give. In Christ's name I pray. Amen.

Give Thanks

Give thanks to the LORD... Who
gives food to all flesh, for His
lovingkindness is everlasting.

PSALM 136:1,25

Dear God, one of the most interesting things to see when I'm sitting quietly in Your great outdoors is a deer feeding on acorns. When the mast is plentiful and the ground is covered with the plump fruit of an oak tree, not only is the sight of a feasting deer enjoyable, so is the muffled sound of the crunching of the shells between their teeth. When a deer lifts its head and looks around as it munches, there seems to be a hint of "thank You" on its face. I pray when You see me (and hear me) enjoying the blessing of a plate of food, You also will see gratefulness on my face. In Your Son's name I pray. Amen.

No Equal

I, the LORD, am the maker of all things,
stretching out the heavens by Myself
and spreading out the earth all alone.

ISAIAH 44:24

God, my awesome Creator, when I'm outdoors there's not a direction I can look that I don't see something You've made that is absolutely astounding. From the tiny speck of dust that sparkles in the beaming ray of a morning sun to the gargantuan sun itself, everything reminds me that You can't be compared to anyone, especially when it comes to Your creative ability. You have no equal. Only You, God, can give such a tangible sign of Your majesty and power as You've provided through Your creation. I will bless Your name now and always for creating me and allowing me to take part in the wonder of You. In Christ's name I pray. Amen.

Fear Leads to Learning

*The fear of the LORD is the
beginning of knowledge.*

PROVERBS 1:7

Dear God, I won't forget how anxious I felt the first time I loaded a muzzleloader and fired a shot. I'd seen videos of an exploding barrel caused by the owner failing to seat the bullet on the charge and the near-death injury it caused. That sobering imagery is what drove me to find out all I could about how to handle this traditional weapon.

When it comes to my relationship with You, I know without a doubt there is none greater or more powerful than You. I want to show You my utmost respect. I know You have the power to destroy both body and soul. Because this is absolutely true, I ask You to help me learn more about You through Your written Word, through prayer, and through fellowship with others whose hearts are filled with reverence for You.

Blessed be Your precious and powerful name! In Christ's name I pray. Amen.

Untethered

On that day, the one who is on the housetop
and whose goods are in the house must not
go down to take them out; and likewise
the one who is in the field must not turn
back. Remember Lot's wife. Whoever
seeks to keep his life will lose it, and
whoever loses his life will preserve it.

LUKE 17:31-33

Father in heaven, I need Your help to daily live with an open-handed attitude when it comes to earthly possessions and connections. I'm grateful for all You've provided for me in this world. But on that day when it's my time to leave the woods of this life and go to the fields of eternity, I don't want to be so tightly tethered to this world that I look back and miss what You've prepared for me in heaven. In Christ's name I pray. Amen.

A Helpful Admission

Christ Jesus came into the world to save sinners, among whom I am foremost of all.

1 TIMOTHY 1:15

Lord, there have been times while I'm hunting that I've messed up and said, "Nobody does it 'worser.'" Maybe I'm not the worst hunter on the planet and my reaction to my blunder is an exaggeration, but just admitting my mistake helps me want to improve. When it comes to the error of sin, sometimes I feel like the apostle Paul, whose depth of regret for his wrongdoing drove him to declare that he was the worst of all sinners. While it may have indeed been an overstatement, perhaps it was his way of motivating himself to a higher standard.

As sorry as I am for my sin, I'm even more grateful that Christ Jesus came to earth to save the worst of sinners. Like Paul, I am in desperate need of redemption, so I seek Your forgiveness for my sin and trust that You came into this world to save me. May it be so—in Your name. Amen.

Guide Service

Listen to counsel and accept discipline,
that you may be wise the rest of your days.

PROVERBS 19:20

Father in heaven, one of the best illustrations of how I should relate to You is found in how I'm expected to relate to hunting guides. I'm required to trust them as they lead me into the wild and then safely back to camp. Their job, as well as their reputation, hinges on their ability to guide, their understanding of the territory, and their knowledge of the game being pursued. Thank You, God, that You have offered to be my Eternal Guide, to lead me spiritually and physically. I know I can trust You, and I gladly follow You. I will listen closely to Your instructions, and I will trust You every step of the way. I know when I do, I will find success because when You guide, Your success rate is 100 percent. You alone are worthy of following without hesitation. Amen.

Fowl Water

*They cried to the L*ORD *in their trouble, and*
He brought them out of their distresses. He
caused the storm to be still, so that the
waves of the sea were hushed. Then they
were glad because they were quiet, so He
guided them to their desired haven.

PSALM 107:28-30

Lord, what an incredible sight and sound when the sky fills with a seemingly innumerable number of ducks or geese. Whenever I'm blessed to be present at their arrival, You know how my soul rejoices. You're also aware that in order to enjoy such an incredible rush of joy, I have to deal with the fact that water is one-half of the word "waterfowl."

When the weather turns nasty and the wind appears to be flipping the lake upside down, I'll be calling on You for help. Only You can deliver my friends and me through the storm. I always give You credit for quieting the waters and for our safe deliverance to our desired haven—our bird blind, where Your hand of protection can be seen.

Blessed be Your mighty name. Amen.

Ask, Seek, Find

Ask, and it will be given to you;
seek, and you will find; knock, and
it will be opened to you.

MATTHEW 7:7

Father in heaven, hunters are not strangers to asking, seeking, and knocking. Asking happens when we say, "Lord, would You let there be antlers?" I admit that prayer always comes out a little awkward because I know in the grand scheme of things it's not all that critical. However, You know I'm dead serious when I ask, "O God, will You help me find this wounded elk?" Seeking is what we do each time we head to the woods, fields, mountains, and waterways to look for game. We're familiar with knocking too. We rap on a farmer's door to get permission to hunt on his or her property. In a spiritual way, I want to be just as diligent to ask, seek, and knock. Thank You for Your promise to give when I ask, to help me find when I seek, and to answer when I knock. You are a blessing beyond measure. Amen.

Confession Is a Weight Lifter

*Confess your sins to one another, and pray
for one another so that you may be healed.*

JAMES 5:16

L ord, I'm awestruck at how relieved I feel when I've confessed a sin to a brother. I'm reminded of how confession of wrongdoing can lighten the burden of guilt when I tell a hunting buddy about a bad shot I made at a deer or other kind of animal. While I know an errant shot isn't usually considered a sin, the remorse and guilt that invade my heart are very real. Without exception, my friend's compassion and understanding help soothe my soul and lift my spirit. It's also a comfort when he says, "I appreciate how bad you feel, but I'm here for you."

It's that kind of listening ear and encouragement I want to offer to anyone who confesses a wrongdoing to me—whether it's a hunter burdened by a wayward shot or a buddy who needs to confess a spiritual transgression. You are compassionate with me, Lord, and I want to pass that compassion on to others. May it be so in Your name and to Your glory. Amen.

One Ambition

We also have as our ambition, whether at
home or absent, to be pleasing to Him.

2 Corinthians 5:9

Father in heaven, I know You're very aware that many hunters who pursue big game have an abiding hope they'll find an animal that qualifies as a trophy for the record books. I admit I can be added to that group. I think about the possibility of getting a "once in a lifetime" animal every time I head to the woods. While it would be very gratifying to accomplish that goal, I don't want to be so obsessed that it negatively affects the rest of my life. The only all-consuming ambition I want to have is the one the apostle Paul had—to please You. I want to live so You are pleased with my integrity and my roles as husband, dad, in-law, friend, and most of all, Your child. I want to please You. In Christ's name I pray. Amen.

Hunters Behind Bars

Remember the prisoners, as though
in prison with them, and those
who are ill-treated, since you
yourselves also are in the body.

HEBREWS 13:3

God, from time to time when I'm sitting quietly at the edge of a field or in a tree stand, or when I'm walking slowly down a logging road, I feel a deep gratitude for the freedom I'm enjoying. It's in those settings that I often think of those who'd love to be where I am at the moment but because of a choice they made that broke a law they are behind bars. My heart breaks for the imprisoned hunter who has a deep ache in his soul because he is locked up. I can't imagine the sadness he feels as autumn approaches and he knows that another season will arrive without the ability to enjoy it.

I pray for every hunter behind bars. And, God, if You open the door for me to be a friend to an incarcerated outdoorsman, help me know what to say and how to encourage him. In the name of Jesus, the only One who can truly free every person, I pray. Amen.

As the End Comes

*The end of all things is near; therefore,
be of sound judgment and sober
spirit for the purpose of prayer.*

1 PETER 4:7

Like the setting sun tells me the end of a day's hunt is coming, Lord, there are signs that tell me the end of all things is near. Because the closing of time is imminent, You want me to make the wise choice to be on the alert so I will remain prayerful. Praying will keep me ready and able to deal with whatever challenges are ahead. It will daily renew my trust in You as this world crumbles around me. Thank You even now for hearing my prayers that I lift up to You. Blessed be Your name! Amen.

They Shoot in the Dark

In the LORD I take refuge...Behold, the
wicked bend the bow, they make ready
their arrow upon the string to shoot
in darkness at the upright in heart.

PSALM 11:1-2

God, this is not the only time in history when those who follow You are targets of the wicked. I don't fully understand why You and those who love You are so hated, but it's a fact of life. When we least expect it, our enemies fire at us from their secret blinds with the intent to destroy our trust in You and to kill our resolve to remain devoted to You.

Whether it's arrows of malicious lies from nonbelievers, accusations of intolerance from people who don't understand Your great love, or the torture and death of believers by Your enemies, I pray for Your protection for all who follow You and worship You in spirit and truth.

Help me, Father, to keep my eyes open for the attacks. Grant me the shield of faith to block the shots against me. I trust You to be the ultimate Victor against the wicked. In the name of Your mighty Son, Jesus, I pray. Amen.

Sure-Footed

If I should say, "My foot has slipped,"
Your lovingkindness, O
LORD, will hold me up.

PSALM 94:18

Lord, You know very well that on the journey of life the trail can sometimes turn steep and treacherous. From health issues to financial woes, from struggles in relationships to difficulties at work, the going can be scary whether I'm heading up a mountain or descending it. I'm very grateful for the promise in Your written Word that if I cry out and say my spiritual or emotional foot has slipped, You will put Your arms of love around me and hold me up so I won't fall. I trust You to do this for me. And each time You do, my confidence in You increases. You are the sure-footed One, and I gladly lean on You. Amen.

Evidence

*Faith is the substance of things hoped
for, the evidence of things not seen.*

HEBREWS 11:1 KJV

How many times, Lord, have I sat in a deer stand imagining a big buck walking my way? I expect him to show up because near my stand is evidence he's in the area. Sometimes it's an unusually large hoof track on a trail or a huge scrape under a licking branch. How grateful I am for exciting encouragements like these.

In this scene is a great illustration of faith. There are things in life outside the woods that I hope for, such as healing for a family member or friend or the provision of something I need. The evidence that You are able and willing to provide what I hope for is found in the signs You've left on the trail through Your Word, the Bible. There are many stories of Your healing power and strength. Each one tells me that even though I can't always see what I hope for, You can bring it about. My faith is in You, O Lord. In Your name I pray. Amen.

Everywhere and Always

*Blessed be the name of the LORD from
this time forth and forever. From
the rising of the sun to its setting the
name of the LORD is to be praised.*

PSALM 113:2-3

Lord, the words of the psalmist that say Your name is to be praised from the rising of the sun to its setting seems to be a reference to a time frame, but it's not that at all. Instead, because the sun is always rising in the east and always setting in the west somewhere, it's a reference to the *place* Your name is to be praised. The *time* for praising You is *forever and always*. From now on, when I'm fortunate enough to hunt from daylight to dark, I will remember that You are to be praised everywhere and all the time. Blessed be Your name right here, right now, and forever.

Special Day

This is the day which the LORD has made;
let us rejoice and be glad in it.

PSALM 118:24

O God and Maker of all things, thank You for making days—especially the notable days that hold such incredible meaning and are causes for celebrating. Hunters, including me, have special days that bring us great joy—the first day we went to the woods, the first hunting trip with a child, and opening day of each new hunting season. None of these, of course, compare to the day You made salvation possible for all of mankind through Jesus Christ. That is the ultimate cause for rejoicing! Because of that day, I am not hopeless. I am forever grateful for the day of Christ, and I will rejoice and be glad in it. In His name I smile and love. Amen.

The Elevated View

> [Zaccheus] climbed up into a sycamore
> tree in order to see [Jesus], for He was
> about to pass through that way. When
> Jesus came to the place, He looked up and
> said to him, "Zaccheus, hurry and come
> down, for today I must stay at your house."
>
> LUKE 19:4-5

Lord, how glad I am that the story of Zaccheus climbing a tree to see You is in Your written Word. His intention was to get above the things that blocked his view so he could get a glimpse of You. That's what a tree stand can do for hunters too. For me, it's a place where I can look beyond the distractions that everyday life yields to get to know You better. When I'm up there, I want to use my waiting time wisely by learning about Your greatness and character that can be seen and understood through Your creation. I know when I connect with You and discover more about You, I'll be a different man when I come down. May it always be so. In Your name, amen.

Jerusalem Prayer

Pray for the peace of Jerusalem:
"May they prosper who love you."

PSALM 122:6

ather of Abraham, Isaac, and Jacob, I live where there is generally peace. Sometimes when I'm enjoying a tranquil place outdoors, I think of countries where there is awful turmoil. One of the nations where the chaos is troublesome is the home of Your precious Jewish people. What a privilege to add my voice to the millions of others who are praying that peace will come to Jerusalem and all of Israel.

I pray Your people will know the peace that You alone can give and that will bring an end to wars and strife. Protect Your beloved ones, God, and open their eyes to You. You promised to prosper those who love Jerusalem, the city that has held the heartbeat of Your people since ancient times. May peace in Jerusalem create an environment where Your gospel of grace and forgiveness through Jesus can be made known without hindrance. In Your Son's name I pray. Amen.

Wheat and Tares

*The kingdom of heaven may be compared
to a man who sowed good seed in his
field. But while his men were sleeping, his
enemy came and sowed tares among the
wheat, and went away… The slaves said
to him, "Do you want us, then, to go and
gather them up?" But he said, "No; for
while you are gathering up the tares, you
may uproot the wheat with them."*

MATTHEW 13:24-25,28-30

God, any hunter who has planted a food plot for game animals or hunted a crop field where the weeds have invaded understands the parable of the wheat and the tares. How unwise to pull up the bad and risk ruining the good, even though it's tempting. When it comes to the church, the devil has planted a few "tares" among us. But Your Word warns that dealing with them harshly might hurt some tender shoots of "wheat." Help me wait patiently for the day when You will separate the good from the bad. Guide me so I will grow in You and be Your wheat forever. In the name of Jesus I pray. Amen.

Feeding on the Good Stuff

*You will be... constantly nourished on
the words of the faith and of the sound
doctrine which you have been following.*

1 Timothy 4:6

God, one of the best reasons to hunt is the quality of meat wild game offers. So much mass-produced food is prepared with chemicals and preservatives that aren't good for me. I'm never totally sure what I'm putting in my body when I eat food bought from grocery stores. When I consume wild game, at least I know what's *not* in it.

In the same way I'm careful about what I feed my body, I'm watchful about the food I feed my spirit. I don't want my diet to include spiritually contaminated or diluted fodder sometimes fed to the masses through some TV shows, movies, news outlets, and social networks. I want to be healthy, not "hellthy."

Thank You for Your Scriptures. I know the teachings from the Bible provide the perfect nourishment. In the name of Jesus, I pray my hunger will always be for You. Feed me daily with Your grace and wisdom. In Christ's name, amen.

Wisdom in the Web

So are the paths of all who forget God;
And the hope of the godless will perish,
Whose confidence is fragile,
And whose trust a spider's web.

JOB 8:13-14

Father, as annoying as spiderwebs can be to walk into when I'm in the woods, there is something useful to learn from them. While a web may be strong enough to capture an insect, it is no match for my flailing arms. Your Word tells me that the confidence of the godless will perish and that whatever they put their trust in will fail them like a fragile strand of a spiderweb. What a great picture of how futile life would be if I chose godlessness. Help me to live a life of godliness, to put my trust in You knowing that if I do, my hope will not perish and my confidence will be strong. In Christ's name I pray. Amen.

Guide Me So I Can Guide Others

He guides me in the paths of
righteousness for His name's sake.

PSALM 23:3

Father in heaven, how grateful I am that You love me enough to show me the trail of righteousness. In the ways that You've done that for me, I want to do for my children and grandchildren. I pray for the courage as a dad and grandfather to take an honest look at the destination my heart is headed and to allow You to reset my course when I stray. I ask this not just for my good, but for the eternal welfare of my kids and grandkids. Continue to lead me in Your ways for Your name's sake, so that I in turn may guide those I love to You. In Jesus' name, may it be so until we are all home with You. Amen.

What a Day That's Coming!

Let the heavens be glad, and let the earth
rejoice; let the sea roar, and all it contains;
let the field exult, and all that is in it.
Then all the trees of the forest will sing for
joy before the LORD, for He is coming.

PSALM 96:11-13

God and Maker of all nature, if I'm still on this earth when You come again, I hope I'm outside when it happens. If I'm granted that privilege, I pray that You will open my eyes to the sight of the heavens showing gladness. I want to see this planet rejoice. I want to hear what it sounds like when the sea and everything that's in it is roaring in anticipation of Your arrival. I long to hear the singing of the forest as You approach. What an incredible day that will be. Come quickly, Lord Jesus! Amen.

Regard for His Blood

How much severer punishment do you
think he will deserve who has trampled
under foot the Son of God, and has
regarded as unclean the blood of the
covenant by which he was sanctified,
and has insulted the Spirit of grace?

HEBREWS 10:29

O God, when I take an animal while hunting, I want to always keep an attitude of respect for its shed blood. I'm aware that it's in that crimson liquid that its life flowed, and spilling it with a casual or cavalier attitude would be unethical. I want to maintain an attitude of respect for that blood for an additional reason. It will help me remember the eternal importance of showing the reverence that is due the blood Jesus shed for my sins when He died on the cross. I never want to think of His blood as unimportant. To do so would insult Him and show contempt for His willingness to sacrifice His very life for the cleansing of my sin-stained soul. Help me always reverence You and Your Son. I ask this in the name of Jesus, my Redeemer. Amen.

Precious Words

Well done, good and faithful servant!

MATTHEW 25:21 NIV

Dear God, there are a lot of words I've enjoyed hearing during my time on earth. The sound of "I love you," the whisper of "We're home," the joy of "Dinner's ready," and the thrill of "Did you just hear a gobble coming from the next hollow?" are just a few. Though these are musical blessings to my ears, when my life is over and I stand before You, I can't think of words I'd rather hear than "Well done, good and faithful servant!" I know that I will hear You say those words because I trust in You and accept Your redemptive grace that comes through Christ. May it be so always. In His name I pray. Amen.

The Risk of Reproach

*Remember the former days, when, after
being enlightened, you endured a great
conflict of sufferings, partly by being made
a public spectacle through reproaches and
tribulations, and partly by becoming
sharers with those who were so treated.*

HEBREWS 10:32-33

Lord, when I discovered how much I enjoy hunting, I didn't realize that sharing the news of my newfound passion would invite some people's contempt. Hatred against hunting and hunters seems to be growing. Even so, I have no plans to muzzle my interest.

I also claim to be Your follower, and that too has inherent hazards. For some fellow believers, the dangers are far worse than I face. I have brothers and sisters around the world who are literally dying because they lay claim to believing in You. Right now I lift them up to You. Grant protection to those who are persecuted for sharing with others their faith in You. Pour courage into their hearts and give them the comfort that only You can give. In the mighty name of Jesus I ask this. Amen.

Hindered, but God Still Wins

We wanted to come to you—I, Paul, more than once—and yet Satan hindered us.

1 THESSALONIANS 2:18

Father in heaven, I may never know until I get to heaven how many times my good intentions were hindered because of the work of the devil. Help me recognize when it is indeed the enemy's hand that is keeping me from doing something I know is part of Your work on earth. If I, like Paul, can identify that hindrance, I'll know better how to pray against it. I ask in advance for You to defeat the tactics of the devil by sending someone to help me succeed in completing Your plans. I believe You will not let Your plans fail when it comes to ministering to those in need. The devil will be defeated. It will be so to Your glory alone. Amen.

Teach Them on the Way

*These words, which I am commanding
you today, shall be on your heart. You shall
teach them diligently to your sons and
shall talk of them when you sit in your
house and when you walk by the way and
when you lie down and when you rise up.*

Deuteronomy 6:6-7

Lord, how grateful I am that Your instructions for where and when to teach children didn't end with "when you sit in your house." Adding "when you walk by the way" is wonderful for someone like me who deeply loves to be outdoors. What an incredible place to show You to my children. There are big rocks I can set them on to tell them how You are the rock of our salvation, trees to let them climb that can be used to talk about the wooden cross where You paid for our salvation, and a gigantic sky to help them understand how big You are. I pray for the wisdom to know how to use these images and innumerable others to spark their interest in You. Again, thank You for the incredible classroom of Your creation. Amen.

Unseen but Real

*The things which are seen are temporal, but
the things which are not seen are eternal.*

2 Corinthians 4:18

O God, I'm astounded when I consider that You put everything I can see in the "temporary" category—even things that have been around for thousands of years, like the sun. If You consider that ancient fireball temporary, then the guy I see when I look in the mirror is definitely short on time. But I have a great hope knowing that as my outer, visible man is decaying, inside the eternal me will someday break free and live forever. When that time comes, I pray You will receive the everlasting me into Your eternal world. I trust it will be so because of Christ, whose love is without end. Amen.

Shell of a Man

May the God of hope fill you with
all joy and peace in believing, so
that you will abound in hope by
the power of the Holy Spirit.

ROMANS 15:13

Shell of a Man

There was no good reason that I could see
Why anything that was everything was taken
    from me
My heart felt like a tomb that was waiting for
    the dead
That's when I went to You and said

"I'm just a shell of a man, Lord
And You know I wish I could bring You more."
But then You said, "Son, you're the one I'm
    looking for
'Cause if I'm gonna give you everything I am
What I need is just a shell of a man"

Giving up so much wasn't easy to do
But it had to be done so You could make room
For the mountain of joy and a river of peace
I'll never forget when I fell on my knees and said

"I'm just a shell of a man, Lord
And You know I wish I could bring You more"
But then You said, "Son, you're the one I'm
      looking for
'Cause if I'm gonna give you everything I am
What I need is just a shell of a man"[3]

Having His Mind

*Who has known the mind of the
Lord, that he will instruct Him?
But we have the mind of Christ.*

1 CORINTHIANS 2:16

God, it's very interesting how a seasoned deer hunter can follow a deer's usual travel route through the woods without a lot of need to closely inspect the trail. As You know, it's because the hunter's instincts have been honed by time and experience, so much so that he or she practically thinks like a deer. They have the mind of the animal. In a similar way, it can be said of those who have followed You for a while and have allowed You to teach them through Your Word, that they have Your mind. That's what I want for my walk with You. I pray that You will continue to instruct me in Your ways so that my spiritual instincts will be keenly tuned to how You think. I know if I do, I won't get lost in the wilderness of this world. Blessed be Your holy name! Amen.

Like an Old Oak

They will still yield fruit in old age.

PSALM 92:14

Father in heaven, every fall when I head back into the woods for archery season, I'm inspired by a particular object of Your creation. It's the huge, aging oak tree that's still producing plump acorns. What a grand sight to behold a plentiful covering of nutty browse for the animals on the forest floor underneath the massive, mature tree. I pray that in my later years I will be as productive as that old, healthy oak. I know the key to being fruitful throughout life is to stay rooted in the rich soil of Your wonderful grace. Thank You for keeping me fed spiritually so I can help feed others. In Christ's name I pray. Amen.

Story in the Bones

*Joseph made the sons of Israel swear, saying,
"God will surely take care of you, and you
shall carry my bones up from here."*

GENESIS 50:25

O God who gives life, when I'm hunting and come upon a skeleton of an animal, it's intriguing to think about what kind of life the creature had, how it survived, what part of the area it favored, and how it died. Bones tell a story. Perhaps Joseph believed that his bones would tell of his God-directed journey—from the pit his brothers threw him into, to the Egyptian palace where he served the Pharaoh—and that's what prompted him to ask that his remains be taken from Egypt to the land he owned near Shechem. It seems he wanted his descendants to know that Egypt wasn't where his heart felt at home. This bone-based illustration of a person's legacy and the impact it can have on those who come afterward compels me to ask, "What would my bones say about me?" Lord, I pray that You will cause me to consider daily the testimony my life and death will leave when people remember me. May it bring You glory. Amen.

Heartfelt Words

*This is My beloved Son, in
whom I am well-pleased.*

Matthew 3:17

Father in heaven, even though Your statement "This is my beloved Son, in whom I am well-pleased" wasn't said directly *to* Jesus, how gratified He must have felt when He heard You say it *about* Him. I can only imagine how deeply it confirmed His relationship with You and empowered Him with confidence. When it comes to my children, borrowing Your words and saying them both *to* them and *about* them helps them feel assured of my love for them and emboldens them with confidence. Thank You for being my Role Model. Amen.

Knowing the Difference

If anyone says to you, "Behold, here is the Christ," or, "There He is," do not believe him. For false Christs and false prophets will arise and will show great signs and wonders, so as to mislead, if possible, even the elect.

MATTHEW 24:23-24

Lord, hunters are familiar with the need to process information accurately. We have to determine if a sound we hear or a mark on the ground we see is from the animal we're seeking. If we fail to determine the source of the sign, the possibility for success plummets. As one who pursues a solid relationship with You, I'm grateful that hunting has helped me understand the importance of correctly interpreting spiritual signs. I want to know the difference between You—the real, living, resurrected Christ—and impostors and false prophets.

Jesus, I ask for the discernment I need to keep from being misled. Please guard my heart and show me how to stay on track by following You and Your Word. May it be so in Your name. Amen.

Ebenezers

Samuel took a stone and set it between
Mizpah and Shen, and named it Ebenezer,
*saying, "Thus far the L*ORD* has helped us."*

1 SAMUEL 7:12

Lord, You know one of the most valuable things hunters have is our memories of past hunts. The remembrances of places I've hunted, as well as what happened in each spot, are peppered across my mind like a herd of pins on a national map. I can go to any one of them and recall details are precious. More than that, they're useful because what I learned in the past can be applied to the present. These hunting memories resemble the much more important recollections I have of the unforgettable times in my life when You've helped me in my journey. Like the Ebenezer stone Samuel set up to remind the people of the help You gave, I have stones of remembrance along my trail that I can point to and declare, "Thus far the Lord has helped me." Thank You, Lord, for being there for me. Blessed be Your name. Amen.

The Big Shock

I delivered to you as of first importance
what I also received, that Christ died
for our sins according to the Scriptures,
and that He was buried, and that
He was raised on the third day.

1 Corinthians 15:3-4

If a hunter hunts long enough, very likely the "big shock" is going to happen. It's the moment when the approach is made toward an animal believed to be dead, but suddenly it jumps up and runs off, never to be seen again. The frustration the hunter feels is mixed with amazement.

Lord Jesus, that must have happened to a lot of people when they found out You had risen from the dead. What a shock to those who refused to believe or didn't realize You were God's Son. Those who hated You were surely angry and scared. And for Your followers, Your resurrection was the most wonderful shock they could imagine. For me, it was a wonderfully astonishing event! The good news is that I, along with a host of others, have the promise You will come again. I don't know exactly when that will be, but I look forward to it. Amen.

A Striking Call to Worship

He covers His hands with the lightning,
and commands it to strike the mark.
Its noise declares His presence.

JOB 36:32-33

Almighty God, what a hair-raising experience to be outdoors when a bolt of lightning suddenly strikes nearby. When it happens, not only can I see the evidence of Your great power, but I also feel the impact of it rumble through my entire body. It's especially amazing to think that such an incredible display of Your boundless energy is only a momentary sample of Your power that has no end. Knowing You command even the lightning encourages me to humbly worship You all the days of my life. Amen.

The Hired Hand

*He who is a hired hand, and not a
shepherd, who is not the owner of
the sheep, sees the wolf coming, and
leaves the sheep and flees, and the wolf
snatches them and scatters them.*

JOHN 10:12

O Father in heaven, You provide a clear picture of
why it's utterly important that parents, when
necessary, find someone who is trustworthy and courageous to watch their children. A weakhearted, self-
centered, stand-in shepherd, who would quickly
abandon the flock if he sees a vicious wolf approaching,
is bad for the sheep and definitely perilous for children.

I pray for parents who find it necessary to enlist
the help of others to care for their little lambs. Give
them the discernment they need to choose wisely.
Give them perseverance to not hire someone if even
the slightest question arises about their integrity and
courage. I pray for Your protection of the children.
They are precious in Your sight, and so are the parents.
Have mercy on them and keep them safe. In Christ's
name I pray. Amen.

Praying for Those Who Pray for Me

God...is my witness as to how unceasingly I
make mention of you, always in my prayers.

ROMANS 1:9-10

Father, how grateful I am for those who have diligently prayed for me through the years. It's a tremendous blessing to know that even when I'm not aware of it, my name is heard in heaven through the loving prayers of friends and family. I won't know until eternity how many times and how many ways I've been blessed because of Your answers to people's prayers. God, I want to pray for those who pray for me. Whether I'm in the quiet of the outdoors or in the midst of a chaotic workday, I ask You to bring them to my mind, especially if they have a particularly pressing need for prayer. Though I may not know why, I trust that You know what they need. What a privilege You give me—to be allowed to bring the needs of people I care about to Your attention. You are a kind and caring heavenly Father. Amen.

What's Done in Secret

*When you fast, anoint your head and
wash your face so that your fasting will
not be noticed by men, but by your Father
who is in secret; and your Father who sees
what is done in secret will reward you.*

MATTHEW 6:17-18

Lord, I am grateful that You wired me to want to hunt. Not only do I love to do it, but it's a great way to provide for something else I love to do—eat. As a confessed "grazer" who likes to partake of the bounty of the earth, the idea of fasting isn't one I readily entertain. Even though I know it can be a very effective addition to my prayers, You know how I struggle to forsake food even for that worthy purpose. Yet You didn't say "*If* you fast;" You said "*When* you fast…" I would be wise to choose fasting as a way to strengthen my prayers. I want to do it right by not openly telling others or complaining about it. Thank You for helping me secretly humble myself in this way. Thank You in advance for the reward You will give for my sacrifice. Amen.

The Travel Companion

*I came today to the spring, and
said, "O LORD, the God of my master
Abraham, if now You will make my
journey on which I go successful…"*

GENESIS 24:42

Dear God, the words of Abraham's servant are mine too. I know that it is wise to desire Your presence with me on the journey of life. You've heard me ask that You grant me safety and success when I enter the woods to hunt, but how much more I need You with me when I'm not hunting. I want the accomplishments You want for me in all areas of my life. From relationships with family to being a good friend, from being a laborer worthy of hire to being Your servant on earth, if You are with me, helping me to do my best, the outcome will be great. Without You, I'll fail. Thank You for loving me enough to invite me to walk with You. In the name of Christ, my truest and most faithful travel companion, I ask these things. Amen.

No Other Help in Battle

LORD, there is no one besides You to
help in the battle between the powerful
and those who have no strength; so help
us, O LORD our God, for we trust in You,
and in Your name have come against
this multitude. O LORD, You are our
God; let not man prevail against You.

2 CHRONICLES 14:11

Just as a young rabbit is no match for the talons of a skilled, mature hawk, or a fawn is helpless when attacked by a massive mountain lion, there are well-meaning but spiritually weak people who are defenseless against an assault by the devil. Lord, I pray that You will step in and be their defense. Strengthen their trust in You. Let them see the victory You can give when they ask for Your help. Let the enemy know that when he comes against Your tender ones, he is coming against You and he will not prevail. And, Lord, when I'm one of those whose strength is gone, I trust You to help me as You have helped others. In Your name I pray. Amen.

Eyes Fixed

*Let us run with endurance the race that
is set before us, fixing our eyes on Jesus.*

HEBREWS 12:1-2

Lord, only You know the number of times I've peered into the dense brush of a thicket and seen what appeared to be a deer's eye, the tip of its ear or tail, or the shape of its leg…but it wasn't. You also know how many times, after intense staring, those signs of wildlife turned out to be real. This is a terrific illustration of what it means to fix my eyes on You. Just as there are potential diversions for me as a hunter to deal with, such as sweat in my eyes, swarming gnats, and gusty wind, life can also create diversions, such as worry, fear, and doubt. I pray for Your strength and grace to help me look past the distractions and focus on You. I bless Your name for making Yourself visible to me through faith. I set my will to keep my eyes fixed on You and Your goodness. In Your Son's name I pray. Amen.

Thanks for Repeaters

*My brethren, rejoice in the Lord. To
write the same things again is no trouble
to me, and it is a safeguard for you.*

PHILIPPIANS 3:1

When it comes to teaching young hunters about safety, repeating instructions is never wrong. No doubt, Lord, it's one of the reasons most of us who hunt are still around. How grateful I am for the seasoned hunter who didn't mind saying things over and over to me, such as, "Don't cross a fence with a gun in your hand," "Check your safety," and "Wear your harness in that tree stand!" His willingness to do so was a sign he cared about me. As a believer in You, Jesus, I'm thankful for those who loved me enough to keep reminding me of things I needed to do to stay spiritually safe. Hearing them say, "Make sure You read God's Word," "Don't forsake assembling with other believers," and "Don't forget to pray" are all welcome evidence that I am loved. I pray for the grace to be a loving repeater of good advice to others as people have been to me. In Your name I pray. Amen.

Sweet Aroma

May my prayer be counted
as incense before You.

PSALM 141:2

The hunter's world is filled with meaningful aromas, Lord. Just a whiff of smoke coming from a wood fire can send me on a journey back to spike camp in the mountains or a cabin where some great memories were made. The wafting smell of roasting venison triggers a longing to go out and make more memories.

I wonder if David's desire that his prayers be considered as incense before You was triggered by how much he loved the smell of a campfire. If so, I agree with him. May my prayers to You bring You as much pleasure as wood smoke brings to me. I rejoice in Your name. Amen.

The Babbler

Epicurean and Stoic philosophers were
conversing with [Paul]. Some were
saying, "What would this idle babbler
wish to say?" Others, "He seems to be a
proclaimer of strange deities,"—because he
was preaching Jesus and the resurrection.

ACTS 17:18

Father, during my years as a hunter, I've had a few encounters with those who consider themselves all-knowing and indisputably correct when it comes to their antihunting stance. I've found that it's fruitless to argue with them because they consider me to be what the philosophers considered Paul to be—a babbler, a scatterer of words with no meaning. All I can do is pray for those who consider my words worthless. The same is true for anyone who thinks I'm a babbler when I tell them about You and the salvation You offer through Your Son's sacrifice on the cross, His time in the grave, and His resurrection. As I speak of Jesus, I trust that the words of truth will bypass their resistant minds and touch their hearts. It's a work that You alone can do. May You receive the glory for the good that is accomplished. Amen.

Watch, Pray, Stay Awake

Keep watching and praying that you may not enter into temptation; the spirit is willing, but the flesh is weak.

MATTHEW 26:41

At times it's not easy to stay awake while in a deer stand. Lord, when the sun You made appears on a cold morning and begins to warm my body, it's not long until my eyes want to droop, my jaw slowly drops involuntarily, and slumber follows. If sleep takes over and I fall forward, what happens can be deadly, especially if there's no safety device involved. I know the only way to avoid this health risk is to stay awake and keep watching. That's the kind of hunter I strive to be. Even more important, Lord, I want to be one of Your followers who keeps my spiritual eyes open so I won't fall into temptation. May it be so to Your glory and my spiritual safety. In Your name I pray. Amen.

The Greater Joy

I have no greater joy than this, to hear
of my children walking in the truth.

3 JOHN 4

ather in heaven, when the apostle John wrote of
the great joy that came with hearing that his children were walking in the truth, I realized he was referring to the children in the faith that he loved. When
I apply this sentiment to my children in the flesh, the
same is true. There really is no greater joy for me than
to hear that they have chosen to follow your Son,
Jesus, who said, "I am the truth." I pray they will continue to walk with Him. Please deliver them from the
evil one whose mission is to see them go astray.

I also pray for parents who are facing the greatest
sadness because their children have chosen the broad
way that leads to destruction. Give these parents the
strength to persevere, and grant the children mercy
and grace so they will turn to You. Save them, O
Father, and bring joy back to the hearts of their moth-
ers and fathers. In the name of Jesus I pray. Amen.

Getting Closer

Draw near to God and He
will draw near to you.

JAMES 4:8

God, every time I go hunting I become an illustration of You drawing near when I reach out to You. I intentionally make the effort to get out of my comfortable bed and make the trip to the place where the wild game is. If I don't go to them, there will be no encounter. The beasts and birds of the field are not going to come strolling into my bedroom for a rendezvous. In a similar way, to experience the comfort as well as the exciting joy of Your presence, I know I need to deliberately draw near to You. I want to get closer to You through prayer, worship, obedience to Your commands, and righteous living. As I do, I trust You to draw near to me. When You do, I will say with the psalmist, "The nearness of God is my good" (Psalm 73:28). Amen.

Come and Drink

On the last day, the great day of the feast,
Jesus stood and cried out, saying, "If anyone
is thirsty, let him come to Me and drink."

JOHN 7:37

O Lord, I can't imagine how intense the thirst is for a deer plagued by the disease that swells their tongue and throat to the point they're unable to drink. How I wish such a painful, devastating condition had never entered into nature. The imagery of a sick animal standing and staring at water it can't swallow is horrifying and heartbreaking.

I wonder if the pity I feel for the poor, diseased deer is similar to how You feel when You see people who are so desperately sick with sin that they struggle to drink from Your streams of grace. I pray that those in this situation will respond to Your invitation and let You satisfy their thirst for forgiveness. May they drink of Your goodness and experience the incredible peace that comes with knowing You intimately. Only You can satisfy their thirsty souls. Amen.

Not by My Might

*The LORD said to Gideon, "The people
who are with you are too many for Me
to give Midian into their hands, for
Israel would become boastful, saying,
'My own power has delivered me.'"*

JUDGES 7:2

What a mistake it would be, Lord, to take full credit for any victory I experience in this life. Whether the battle is fought physically or spiritually, if there's triumph, I know when I look closely I'll see Your hand in the outcome. Help me to never boastfully claim a success I know in my heart is Yours. Instead, open my eyes to see how, when, and where You fought for me so I may boldly testify of Your power that delivered me. In the mighty and matchless name of Jesus, amen.

Faithful Wounds

Faithful are the wounds of a friend.

PROVERBS 27:6

How grateful I am, O Lord, for my hunting friends. You know how beneficial it is to my soul when I get to engage in humor and kidding around with them. The value of their friendship goes beyond the fun though. When friends detect an attitude in me that isn't good and discern that it could lead me down a harmful path, their bold willingness to point it out is such a great blessing, even if it stings to hear their challenges. In those times, I realize I have the truest of friends. I pray for the grace to always accept their brave love. I also pray that when my turn comes to be that kind of faithful friend to them that You'll give me the strong heart to be just as courageous. In Your loving name I pray. Amen.

Music to His Ears

I will sing of the lovingkindness of the LORD
forever; to all generations I will make
known Your faithfulness with my mouth.

<small>PSALM 89:1</small>

Father in heaven, You know how excited I feel when I get to go hunting. You also know how eager I am to tell stories of successful hunts to anyone who will listen. I want to be just as enthused when I tell others, especially those I love, about Your faithfulness and the boundless love You've shown so clearly to me through the years. May the words of my mouth be music to Your ears as I testify of Your greatness. May my songs of praise bring You the glory You deserve. I ask this in the thrilling name of Jesus. Amen.

Familiar Words

*To Him who is able to keep you from
stumbling, and to make you stand in
the presence of His glory blameless with
great joy, to the only God our Savior,
through Jesus Christ our Lord, be glory,
majesty, dominion and authority.*

JUDE 24-25

Father, the words in this passage are familiar to me as a hunter. I sometimes *stumble* when entering and exiting the woods in the dark. I often go to my *stand* to watch and wait. I experience great *joy* as I see the *glory* and the *majesty* of Your creation. I have been given *dominion* over the animals, and the uniformed folks who drive the green trucks have *authority* over me.

Thank You for revealing Yourself and Your awesome attributes to me in this way. You alone have dominion over all. One day, every knee will bow and every tongue confess that You alone have authority to rule the universe. I trust You to keep me from stumbling so I can someday stand in Your presence, forgiven and with great joy. Blessed be Your name forever. Amen.

High Thoughts

*Set your mind on the things above, not
on the things that are on earth.*

Colossians 3:2

Lord, those of us who are serious about chasing gobblers in the spring don't have to wonder what it means to set our minds on things above. The night before a turkey hunt, our sleep is delayed by thoughts that are skyward. We think about what trees the "longbeards" might be roosted in and where we need to be set up when they fly down the next morning. As a turkey hunter, I thank You, Lord, for a helpful illustration of setting my mind on things above. As Your child, I want my thoughts to often be heavenward, where You now sit on Your throne and intercede for those who follow You. I want to remember that You came down to earth, with Your great compassion You blotted out my many transgressions, and with Your shed blood You washed away my iniquities. Blessed be Your name, which alone is high and mighty. Amen.

Now the Work Begins

He who steals must steal no longer;
but rather he must labor, performing
with his own hands what is good, so
that he will have something to
share with one who has need.

EPHESIANS 4:28

ord, I'm sure You've heard hunters like me say
many times after a big animal is down, "Now the
work begins!" How true that much labor is involved
in finishing the process of harvesting a kill. But all that
work is overshadowed by the joy of sharing the fruit
of our efforts with family and friends. In Your written
instructions on how we should live, You clearly say
we are not to steal. Instead, we are to work for what
we need and want—and for more reasons than just
staying out of trouble. We will discover the joy that
comes with sharing the rightly gained bounty with
those who might not be able to work for their sustenance. In Christ's name I pray that You'll help me to
always remember to say with joy in my heart, "Now
the work begins!" Amen.

Staying on the Stand

*I am amazed that you are so quickly
deserting Him who called you by the
grace of Christ, for a different gospel.*

GALATIANS 1:6

How many times, Lord, have I been sitting in a deer stand or against a tree while turkey hunting and decided to give up—but then learned the hard way that I should have stayed. The sudden crashing of a fleeing deer that I didn't know was there or the shocking, loud cluck of a nervous, escaping gobbler I didn't see always makes me wish I'd been more patient. With this in mind, I pray for the strength and endurance to be faithful to You, to not be quick to give up on the call You made to me when You invited me to accept Your grace and salvation. I definitely don't want to abandon Your eternal truths for any teachings that would lead me away from You. May it be so for the sake of the salvation of my soul and for the building up of Your kingdom. I pray this in Your name. Amen.

Plans Change

*Do not boast about tomorrow,
for you do not know what a
day may bring forth.*

PROVERBS 27:1

Lord, You know that the only thing predictable about tomorrow's hunt is that nothing about it is predictable. Sure, I have my plans about where I'll go and how long I'll stay, but how quickly my agenda can change because of anything from traffic delays to unexpected bad weather to a jammed gun. And when it comes to the animals, I've been fooled enough by their smarts to know I can't accurately read their minds. To be honest, Lord, I actually prefer it this way because if hunting were totally predictable, why do it? You've made all of life the same as a day in the woods. It sure makes living here interesting.

Because only You know what will happen in a day, I don't want to boast about plans I have. Instead, I want to boast in the fact that I know You, that You know what's in my tomorrow, and You are going to guide me safely to it and through it. Blessed be Your absolutely wonderful name. Amen.

The Gate

Open to me the gates of righteousness;
I shall enter through them, I shall give
thanks to the LORD. This is the gate of the
LORD; the righteous will enter through it.

PSALM 118:19-20

Like I've done many times through the years, Lord,
I will find it necessary in the future to open a gate
to enter a farmer's property where I'm allowed and
privileged to spend the day in the woods. Each time
I do can be a reminder of the psalmist's reference to
the "gate of the LORD" through which those who are
being made righteous by believing in You can enter
into Your presence. There we can spend not just a day
with You, but eternity. What an incredible blessing to
be welcomed on Your property. You are the kindest
of "land owners." And just as I don't take a farmer's
blessing to walk on his or her land for granted, I consider Your permission to walk on Your property to be
valuable beyond measure. Thank You, O God, for the
privilege. In Christ's name I pray. Amen.

Fruitful Evidence

You will know them by their fruits.
Grapes are not gathered from thorn
bushes nor figs from thistles, are they?

Matthew 7:16

God, You've made it very clear in Your Word that the fruit I bear will identify who I really am. You've also shown me this absolute truth in Your incredible creation. When I'm in the woods and see a persimmon on the ground, I don't have to wonder what kind of tree I'm standing under. Not even for a moment do I expect to look up and see a big white oak. And if I see acorns strewn on the forest floor, I know I'm not by an apple tree. Thank You for showing me in this way what it means to be known by my fruit. I pray that I will always bear the evidence of Your presence in my life. I want those who see me to know without a doubt that I belong to You. May it be so to Your glory, in the name of Jesus, who alone causes me to bear good fruit. Amen.

The Memory of Me

The memory of the righteous is blessed,
but the name of the wicked will rot.

PROVERBS 10:7

Father in heaven, there are names of people who come to my mind that bring with them the warmest feelings. Some of them are my hunting buddies, and the reasons I smile when I think of their names are the quality of people they are and the great memories we created together. You know, however, that there are other names that don't generate such good thoughts when they cross my mind. Some of those are also hunters. O God, I know it's only by Your grace that I can live in a way that will keep the taste of my memory sweet in the minds of others. May it be so to Your glory and in Your name, which is above all names. Amen.

Everyone in Me

Bless the LORD, O my soul,
and all that is within me,
bless His holy name.

PSALM 103:1

O Father in heaven, when I see a deer, a duck, a bear, or any other animal, I realize that within each one of them is more of the same species. When the psalmist said, "All that is within me, bless His holy name," I wonder if he was referring to the children he would father as well as the children of his children. Whether or not that thought was on David's mind, it's how I see it. For that reason, it's my sincere prayer that all that is within me—my children, grandchildren, great- and great-great-grandchildren give You the honor that You so deserve. To Your glory and honor I pray. Amen.

Which Way Do I Go?

Without faith it is impossible to please Him.

HEBREWS 11:6

Lord, in those times when I arrive at a place to hunt, get out of my vehicle, and stand looking at the area without knowing exactly which direction I will go, I'm painting a picture of what it means to live by faith. In life, sometimes I feel that way—sort of like Abraham, who went out "not knowing where he was going." He had to trust You to guide him. I'm no different. I always want to put my faith in Your ability to guide me to the place You want me to go. If that doesn't happen, everything I do will be in vain, and my life will not be pleasing to You. Today I ask You to show me where to walk. And if I head in the wrong direction, please redirect my steps. I want this for Your glory and for the good of those I love. In Your name I pray. Amen.

A Single Purpose

*Our fellowship is with the Father,
and with His Son Jesus Christ.*

1 John 1:3

Heavenly Father, sometimes early in the morning, as the sun is coming up on another day of hunting, I think of the others who are doing the same thing I am—basking in the glow of first light. I'm sitting in an outdoor sanctuary that spreads across the nation. Hunters sit in portable climbers, stools inside pop-up blinds, padded chairs in elevated shooting boxes, benches in duck blinds, and even five-gallon plastic buckets. As we wait for the action to begin, we're fellowshipping around a single purpose.

When Sunday comes and Your people gather, the picture is the same. Some folks are in wooden pews or on padded folding chairs, some are on hard benches made of old lumber, others may be sitting on dirt, but we're all doing one thing—entering into fellowship with You, with Your Son, Jesus, and with Your Holy Spirit. May You always be the reason we gather. In Your Son's name I pray. Amen.

Chimneys

*Trust in the LORD forever, for in GOD
the LORD, we have an everlasting Rock.*

ISAIAH 26:4

God, sometimes when I'm out hunting, I'll come upon a site where there was once a house, but everything has crumbled except the stone chimney. That's when I think of You. You're definitely not pictured in the remains of the rotting old wood that has failed to last. Instead, You're like the enduring stand of well-placed, well-chosen stone that has withstood the years of intense heat, the ravages of time, and many destructive storms.

That's who You are, who You were, and who You always will be. Thank You for being trustworthy, strong, and ever-present. Thank You for being available to give me comfort when I need it. Blessed be Your name forever. Amen.

From My Youth

For You are my hope; O Lord GOD,
You are my confidence from my youth.

PSALM 71:5

O God, You above all know that the world is in an incredibly turbulent time. I'm deeply concerned for those I love, but I have a special burden on my heart for the very young ones among us and in the world. The nation they're growing up in is not the same that I knew as a youngster. I remember a calmer, more peaceful time when the level of worry about personal and national safety was hardly a concern. It's a sad situation on the globe now, and the only hope our young ones have is You. Help me do all I can to show them that real peace in the midst of the storms comes only in trusting in Your promise that says, "Whoever believes in Him shall not perish, but have eternal life." I know this truth will carry them through these chaotic times because it's sustaining me. When all is said and done, and time is no more, I pray that they'll be able to look back and say with the psalmist, "You are my confidence from my youth."

The Relief of Rain

I shall give you rains in their season.

LEVITICUS 26:4

I've seen some seasons, Lord, when the earth was so dry that the fallen leaves crunching under my boots felt and sounded like I was walking on cornflakes. I've seen creeks that normally flowed year-round become nothing more than cracks in the earth. I could almost hear the ground crying out for revitalizing rain. Then it came. I've been there when the rainfall began and heard the steady hissing made by countless drops of water. The sound was like a sustained sigh of relief coming from the earth.

Jesus, You know there are times I too have experienced spiritual drought. My soul had gone dry. You knew it well, and You sent the welcomed rain of Your grace. It fell on me through love and prayers from family and friends, insights from Your Word, and timely reminders of Your presence through Your creation. Thank You for the rain that renews, restores, and reminds me that You love me. Amen.

Test First?

Do not be surprised at the fiery
ordeal among you, which comes
upon you for your testing.

1 Peter 4:12

Father, in school I was taught a lesson and then tested on it. I've discovered You often have a different and more productive way of teaching. Sometimes You *test first* and then teach the lesson. I've seen You do this when hunting. It's happened when I was surprised by the sudden appearance of a poisonous snake. It taught me how to defend myself against the danger and schooled me on the need to be more careful about where and how I walked.

Beyond the classroom of the woods, I can see this teaching technique as well. Sudden sickness can test my willingness to trust You to heal. Unexpected financial strain can teach me to understand and trust that You are my provider. And even a "We interrupt our regular programming for this special news bulletin" can surprise me into learning to lean on You for security.

God, I pray for Your help to learn through Your testing so my life will be more satisfying and more pleasing to You. In the name of Jesus I pray. Amen.

Biblically Correct

Do not add to His words or He will
reprove you, and you will be proved a liar.

PROVERBS 30:6

Lord, it's troublesome to hear how many of Your life-changing truths are being watered down by rewording or adding words for the sake of not offending anyone. Someone might paraphrase Romans 3:23, "Everyone has misguided intentions and has not reached their full potential" instead of quoting, "All have sinned and fall short of the glory of God." They seem to want to avoid bringing up the real problem, which is sin.

I don't want to be guilty of diluting Your eternal truths in any way. I need Your help to be bold enough to say things the way You want them said, yet to do so with compassion and confidence so Your Word will accomplish the purpose You intend. I want to draw people to You with open hearts. In Jesus' name I ask for Your help to do this. Amen.

Many Members, One Purpose

*God has placed the members, each one
of them, in the body, just as He desired.
If they were all one member, where
would the body be? But now there
are many members, but one body.*

1 CORINTHIANS 12:18-20

God and Maker of us all, in the archery shot You've provided a great illustration of the need for a body to have many members in order to function well and accomplish its purpose. If I were only a hand, I could do nothing but hold the bow. If I only had an arm (without the shoulder), I couldn't lift the bow. If I were an eye, I could only see the target. If I were a head, all I could do is think about the shot.

When it comes to Your church, every believer in Jesus is needed to fulfill its purpose. The church needs good minds to study and teach, strong arms to lift each other's burdens, steady hands to hold each other in times of grief, and confident feet to carry the good news to those who need hope. Help me, Father, to do my part to build Your kingdom here on earth. In Jesus' name I pray. Amen.

The Cup of Weakness

Most gladly, therefore, I will rather
boast about my weaknesses, so that the
power of Christ may dwell in me.

2 CORINTHIANS 12:9

God, even though my weaknesses are known by You, I'm so grateful they don't cause You to think less of me. Instead, according to Your Word, You see my frailties as potential containers of Your strength. In order for a weakness to become a cup for Your power, I have to admit that it's an area of my life where I lack strength. As a hunter, to get help from a buddy to drag a heavy deer out of the woods, I have to admit I'm in need of the assistance of his muscles. As Your follower, God, I have to be willing to recognize my inabilities and call on You to fill me with Your strength. I do that right now. I trust that You will keep Your promise to dwell in me so that I can continue to walk strongly with You. Thank You for hearing my prayer. Amen.

Small Leads to Big

*He who is faithful in a very little
thing is faithful also in much.*

LUKE 16:10

Lord, when I look back through my years of hunting, I see how being faithful in small things led to bigger things. When I was first learning to hunt, I slept, drank, and ate anything having to do with small game. I studied the behavior of squirrels and rabbits. I learned where they preferred to nest and got very familiar with the sounds they made. Because I was faithful to learn everything I could about them, I was better prepared to begin hunting big game.

I know it works the same way in my spiritual life. When I'm faithful in small things, like giving regularly to the church, I will discover the joy and value of giving even more for God's work. When I'm faithful in being honest in little things, such as putting in a full day's work, I will be trusted with greater responsibilities for God's glory. Lord, help me succeed in being faithful in the small things so I will be ready for the big ones You have planned. In Your name I pray. Amen.

Them over Me

*Do not merely look out for your own
personal interests, but also for the
interests of others. Have this attitude in
yourselves which was also in Christ Jesus.*

PHILIPPIANS 2:4-5

Lord, if given the choice between eating and hunting, I'd rather hunt. This indicates how much I like to hunt and how tempting it is to forget about everyone else and focus on my passion. I know You want me to keep a healthy balance between my love for You, my love for my family, and my desire to hunt. Because I want to please You, I'm asking for Your help. I'm aware I have to deliberately choose to put the interests of my loved ones above my own, but I need Your grace and strength to do so. I see the outcome of my mistakes on the faces of those I've let down. Please forgive me when I fail. By giving Your own life on the cross, You've taught me how to abandon my own interests. Thank You for being my Guide and leading me in this attitude. In Your Son's name I pray. Amen.

Taking Aim

How long will you love what is
worthless and aim at deception?

PSALM 4:2

Thank You, Lord, for the many life-changing insights I can glean from being a hunter. One of the most important hunting-related lessons I can apply to my spiritual life has to do with aiming my weapon. It is imperative that I carefully consider what I'm aiming at when preparing to shoot. Whatever is beyond my gun barrel or tip of my broadhead must be known. If the recipient of my bullet or broadhead is human, I could be guilty of maiming or, worse, killing someone.

Spiritually speaking, I know I need to give great attention to what I'm aiming at in life. If my sights are set on worthless things, such as riches, satisfying lust, or seeking worldly power, and I deceive people to obtain them, I'll be the one who will be pierced and wounded by the projectile of sin. Lord, help me seriously think about where I'm directing my intentions and my desires. I want my aim to always be focused on pleasing You. May this come to pass each day I live. In Your name I pray. Amen.

Hold Fast

Love the LORD your God… walk in
all His ways and hold fast to Him.

DEUTERONOMY 11:22

Lord, how grateful I am for the modern machine called a four-wheeler. In my experience as a hunter, there's no way to measure how much sweat and effort such a useful workhorse saves. What a blessing. I'm also thankful for what the four-wheeler teaches me about my need to hold fast to You. It's a lesson that's learned when two people are riding together. When the gas is applied and the powerful motor makes the machine quickly lurch forward, the passenger better be clutching the driver. If not, the rider will shoot right off the back. Been there, done that, Lord. And the memory is a reminder that I need to acknowledge that You're in control and I desperately need to hold on to You. If I don't, life will dump me. Help me hang on tight, O Lord, especially these days when the world seems to be lunging toward chaos. In the name of Jesus I pray. Amen.

A Gift Received Is a Gift to Give

*Each of you should use whatever gift you
have received to serve others, as faithful
stewards of God's grace in its various forms.*

1 PETER 4:10 NIV

Father in heaven, when You give me a gift, I'm not to hold on to it for my own benefit, but rather to use it to serve others.

My propensity for hunting is a gift from You because it benefits me in many ways. To name a few, the solitude and quiet help me recharge, the challenge keeps boredom at bay, the skills hone my senses, and sharing the activity cultivates friendships. As beneficial as hunting is to me, I'm aware through Your Word that You want me to employ it to serve others. From gathering healthy food for a needy family to showing someone valuable spiritual lessons discovered through experiencing Your creation, the opportunities are there to seize. Help me be a good steward of this gift. May my use of it be pleasing to You. I pray Your grace will be multiplied in the lives of others through this gift You graciously allow me to share. In Your Son's name I ask this. Amen.

Winning by Dying

When He had disarmed the rulers and authorities, He made a public display of them, having triumphed over them through Him.

COLOSSIANS 2:15

Jesus, if all the hunters on the planet gathered with their guns, bows and arrows, and spears, and we pooled our collective skills for finding and killing, we could not defeat the evil one. That reality makes it all the more awe-inspiring to think that You alone defeated him, and how utterly incredible that You did it by dying. I will be forever grateful for Your sacrifice on the cross. Through Your shed blood, You conquered and disarmed the devil and the powers of hell. How comforting to know that I worship and serve the One who alone is triumphant over all evil. What a blessing to be on Your side. Amen.

Spit on Me

*"While I am in the world, I am the Light of
the world." When He had said this, He spat
on the ground, and made clay of the spittle,
and applied the clay to his eyes, and said
to him, "Go, wash in the pool of Siloam"
(which is translated, Sent). So he went
away and washed, and came back seeing.*

JOHN 9:5-7

Jesus, only You can spit on the ground, make a little clay, rub it on a blind man's eyes, tell him to go wash in a pool, and have the man's sight return. The entire scene is incredibly intriguing. I find one part especially interesting because all of mankind can be seen in it. We are like the clay. Actually, we *are* the clay. Alone we can't do much other then take up space and be trampled on by passing feet. But when You connect with us, we become something usable in Your hands. That's what I want for my life. I invite You to spit on me, so to speak, with Your grace, Your Spirit, and Your strength. Make me a healing compound for those You touch with me. In Your name I pray. Amen.

Hang Time

*You do not know what your life will be like
tomorrow. You are just a vapor that appears
for a little while and then vanishes away.*

JAMES 4:14

When I exhale on a chilly morning in the woods, my breath makes a grayish, nearly transparent mist. That's my life. Like that vapor, I appear, hang around a little while, and then vanish. Father in heaven, it's my hang time that I'm praying about today. I know that compared to the span of the ages, my existence on earth is a mere moment, but I don't want to waste it. I want my little piece of time to count for good. For that to happen, I need You to fill my heart with Your grace, which inspires me to show grace. I need Your love that teaches me how to love and serve others. And I definitely need Your forgiveness that compels me to forgive as I've been forgiven. If these requests are granted, I will not have lived in vain. Thanks for hearing the desires of my heart. Amen.

Faithfully Following You

The Son can do nothing of Himself, unless
it is something He sees the Father doing.

John 5:19

Faithfully Follow You

Until I take my last breath
Until I take my last step
Until I close my eyes in death
I want to follow You

Until the setting of my sun
Until my work on earth is done
Until my race on earth is run
I want to follow You

I want to go where I see You go
I want to say what I hear You say
I want to do what I see You do
I want to follow You, faithfully follow You[4]

Maintaining the Temporary Temple

Bodily discipline is only of little profit.

1 TIMOTHY 4:8

Thank You, Father, for Your provision of my earthly body. I know it is a temporary temple of Your Holy Spirit and a testament to Your marvelous creative power. Help me to make it as fit as possible for my journey with You on the trail of this life. Help me be a role model of the value of self-discipline. I see that You didn't say in Your written Word that "bodily discipline [exercise] profits nothing"; instead, it says "bodily discipline is only of little profit." I want to keep my body healthy so I can better serve You. For that reason, I commit today to bring my body under control and treat it like the divine gift it is. By Your grace and strength this will be done. Amen.

Peculiar People

[You] are a chosen generation, a royal
priesthood, a holy nation, a peculiar people.

1 Peter 2:9 kjv

Lord, I'm very sure You know that if a nonhunter is standing close enough to a group of hunters and hears the conversation, it's likely that some of the words will sound odd. Terms like "drop tine," "broadhead," "strutter," "field dress," "comeback call," and "scrape," could leave him scratching his head. Our verbiage is indeed a tip-off that we're a peculiar bunch, but it's a reputation that puts us in good company. Your people are a special group too. If people who knew nothing about Your church were suddenly placed in the midst of a congregation, they might hear terminology that would bewilder them, including "born again," "sanctified," "foot washing," "under conviction," and "freewill offering." I pray for Your people right now, that we will not be afraid or ashamed to be different. Just as blaze-orange makes hunters visible against a bland background of winter deadness, the uniqueness of Your people makes us immediately recognizable in a world deadened by sin. In Your uniquely glorious name I pray. Amen.

Straight to the Table

Enter His gates with thanksgiving
and His courts with praise.
Give thanks to Him, bless His name.

PSALM 100:4

O God, if I were invited to a friend's house to enjoy a meal made from the bounty of his hunt, and without saying a word walked right by him when he opened the door, went straight to his dining room, sat down, and started eating, it would be downright rude. Unfortunately, too many times that's what happens when I pray. I arrive at Your place and, without pausing to say thanks for inviting me in, I go straight to Your table and dig in. Forgive me for the times I've done this. Help me always remember to enter Your gates with a thankful heart for the privilege of being blessed to sit at Your table. In the gracious name of Jesus Christ I pray. Amen.

The Sudden Appearance

You also must be ready; for the
Son of Man is coming at an hour
when you do not think He will.

MATTHEW 24:44

It's uncanny how a sizable animal such as a white-tail deer, an elk, or bear can just appear seemingly out of nowhere. One moment they're not there and the next they are. God, when You created these beasts, You obviously wired them with the ability to slip through their world quietly. Their unexpected, sudden appearance can especially be unnerving when I realize they're looking right at me. What a picture this is of the eventual, sudden appearance You'll make when You return. Unlike the times when I've not been ready for the abrupt presence of an animal, I want to be prepared for Your arrival. Deliver me, Lord, from anything that would hinder my readiness. I know it's by Your grace alone that I won't be caught off guard when You appear. Amen.

"Lazy"—Another Word for Hungry

The lazy do not roast any game, but the diligent feed on the riches of the hunt.

PROVERBS 12:27 NIV

Lord, when it comes to why hunters make the effort to go to where the game is, a fellow hunter said it best: "You must be present to win!" There are two words for getting up really early, enduring the elements for hours on end, and walking for miles for the sake of catching food: "hard work." There is one word for the one who prefers to avoid the work and have the game served to him: "lazy." Of course, Lord, "lazy" is another word for hungry. Lord, of all things I don't want to be accused of, it's being lazy. I prefer the wealth of provision, so for that reason I'll get up off my couch and expend sweat and blood for the sake of catching prey. May my hard work be pleasing to You because, after all, You're always working hard to make all things work for the good of those who love You. Amen.

Armored Up

Be strong in the Lord and in his
mighty power. Put on the full armor
of God, so that you can take your
stand against the devil's schemes.

EPHESIANS 6:10-11 NIV

Lord, getting ready to go hunting is a lot like donning the armor God provides for battling the enemy of my soul. Like an ammo belt, the belt of truth holds powerful rounds to defend myself against Satan's lies. My wind-resistant camo coat is like the breastplate of righteousness that protects me from the bitter cold of evil and sin. My heavy-duty boots are like having my feet "fitted with the readiness that comes from the gospel of peace," prepared to tramp through any terrain to spread the good news of Your presence. My safety harness represents the shield of faith that deflects the deadly arrows of the devil's deception. My hat saves me from the blinding rain and sun and is a picture of the helmet of salvation that keeps me protected while I walk the narrow way to heaven. My loaded weapon is like the sword of God's Word. What a great reason to get dressed to go hunting! Thank You, Lord. Amen.

The Distraction of Action

*Fathers, do not provoke your children
to anger, but bring them up in the
discipline and instruction of the Lord.*

EPHESIANS 6:4

Lord, You have commanded fathers to nurture and instruct their kids. For me, one great way to do this is to take them outdoors. Going to and from the hunter's woods with a son or daughter usually requires some walking, and that provides a perfect setting for instruction and listening. Getting up early, as we hunters usually do, gives us precious, uninterrupted opportunity to connect over a predawn breakfast and while driving to a farm and going back home. Thanks for the freedom to be an "on the go" kind of teacher, Lord. I'll be as diligent as I can to use the "distraction of action" to instruct them in Your ways. Amen.

The Divine Rebuilder

Come, let us rebuild the wall of Jerusalem
so that we will no longer be a reproach.

NEHEMIAH 2:17

Heavenly Father, You made Jerusalem the symbol of Your dwelling, but how sad it was when the walls around it fell at the hands of invaders. Though the testimony to the strength of the city had crumbled, You didn't abandon Jerusalem. Instead, Nehemiah became Your man to rebuild the walls. In my life, there have been times when my defenses have crumbled away, destroyed by bad choices and, worse, a preference for sin over sanctification. But thanks to You, Jesus came with His nail-scarred hands to rebuild the wall around my heart, to restore the strength in me that I need to do Your will, and to renew my purpose in life. You are not just a great builder—You are also a very compassionate and patient rebuilder. Blessed be Your name. Amen.

Lost and Found

I tell you, there is joy in the presence of the angels of God over one sinner who repents.

LUKE 15:10

Lord, hunters aren't exempt from losing things when we're outdoors. Cell phones, car keys, knives with sentimental value, favorite game calls, money, medicine, and on and on the list could go. But oh, how great the relief is to find the thing that our souls grind over because of losing it. The immense happiness we feel in that moment is a very good reminder of a joy that is much, much greater. It's the joy that was expressed in heaven in the presence of the angels when I repented of my sins and gave my life to You. How glad I am to know that though I was lost, now I'm found in You—and it made heaven really happy. I rejoice with the angels. I declare with my whole heart, "Worthy is the Lamb who was slain for my redemption." Amen!

Divine Hyperbole

They came out, they and all their armies with them, as many people as the sand that is on the seashore, with very many horses and chariots.

JOSHUA 11:4

One thing hunters are good at, Lord, is embellishing reality. We say things like "He was a monster buck," or "There must've been a million ducks." Because we're good at enlarging the facts for the sake of storytelling, we understand "as many as the sand that is on the seashore" to describe the size of the army coming against Israel. The hyperbole was to help Your people appreciate the impact of the situation. Of the many grand statements in Your Word, there's one about You that I'm grateful is very accurate: "For God so loved the world, that He gave His only begotten Son, that whoever believes in Him shall not perish, but have eternal life." You loved *everyone* who was, and is, and will be on this planet so much that You gave us Jesus to believe in so we can have a real relationship with You and a life worth living. That's quite a claim—and I believe every word of it! Amen.

I Will!

Who will stand up for me against evildoers?
Who will take his stand for me
against those who do wickedness?

PSALM 94:16

Lord God, my response to these challenging questions asked by the psalmist is, I will. I know it may cost me to stand against evildoers and those who devise wickedness, but to stand with You, O Lord, is to stand on the side of righteousness. Pour Your courage into me, and grant me the privilege of defending Your cause here on earth. Speak through me, Lord. Fill my mouth with bold declarations of Your truth. As You use me, shine the light of Your love and compassion through my eyes to those who are in need of them. I want to be there for You as You have been there for me. Blessed be Your name that is so worthy of defending. Amen.

A Home for the Lonely

God makes a home for the lonely.

PSALM 68:6

Lord, there's hardly anything more tender to see in the wild than a spotted fawn lying quietly in the tall grass on a spring day. If I'm seeing it and the mother isn't in sight, I can count on her being nearby and returning soon. How sad, however, when I discover the fawn's mom isn't coming back because she was the victim of a predator attack or an impact with a truck bumper. If so, it's time for the fawn to get a new home. To leave it alone and lonely wouldn't give it the best chance for survival. Lord, that's what You do for people who have been abandoned. You make homes for the lonely. I pray today that You will have mercy on those who are yet to be given a home. May they encounter Your compassion, and if it is to come through me, show me how, Lord. Help me be Your hand of hope to them. In the name of Christ Jesus, amen.

Treasures

One generation shall praise Your works to
another, and shall declare Your mighty acts.

PSALM 145:4

Treasures

Thank You, Lord, I've seen my children's children
Heaven's love in flesh and bone
How sweet it is to hear them laughing
Where it's been quiet far too long

And, Lord, how I love to take them fishing
And play some catch out in the field
When they talk, I'll be sure to listen
And help them learn to do Your will

Lord I pray for these treasures
You have given to my years
Until they meet You in forever
Take their hand and keep them near

Lord, I pray when they get older
And my name comes to their mind
May this one thing they remember
They saw Your blessed face in mine[5]

Prayer for My Child

*I prayed for this child, and the L*ORD
has granted me what I asked of him.

1 SAMUEL 1:27 NIV

Prayer for My Child

Father God, to You I come
In the name of Your Son
I bring my children to Your throne
Father, hear my cry

Above all else, Lord, save their souls
Draw them near You; keep them close
Be the shield against their foes
Make them Yours, not mine

Give them peace in Christ alone
In their sorrow be their song
No other joy will last as long
Father, calm their fears

Guide their feet, Lord, light their path
May their eyes on You be cast
Give their hands a kingdom task
A purpose for their years

And as my flesh cries out for bread
May I hunger, Lord, instead
That my children would be fed
On Your words of life

So, Father God, to You I come
In the name of Your Son
I bring my children to Your throne
Father, hear my cry[6]

Even a Toothpick

*In the beginning God created
the heavens and the earth.*

GENESIS 1:1

For the record, God, I for one believe, with not even a hint of a shadow of doubt, that You and You alone created the heavens and the earth. To believe that all I see—from the vastness of the sky above my head to the tiniest speck of sand below my feet—was a product of happenstance would be foolish. In fact, I'd need a lot more faith to believe that this universe is a result of random happenstance than I need to accept the idea that it was divinely designed. Even the making of a simple, wooden toothpick requires a blueprint for man to do. This universe, which You made, is no different. And in regard to the toothpick, the truth is, without the intelligent mind (which You made) and the tree (which You also created), neither the blueprint nor the toothpick would exist. You've made an incredible place for us to live and experience the awesomeness of Your creative power. I hope someday You'll let me see how You did it. Amen.

True Friends

*A friend loves at all times, and a
brother is born for adversity.*

PROVERBS 17:17

How thankful I am, O Lord, for hunting buddies who have been helpful when I needed them. What a blessing it is to have an extra pair of eyes to help me find a wounded deer, another strong back to help me get my vehicle out of a ditch, or more important, to put their arm around me when I'm sad or facing troubling times. Friendship was Your idea, Father, and I praise You for it. I pray that You will open my eyes to the needs of my brothers and grant me the strength and wisdom to know how to help them. It's one of the reasons I was born, and I want to fulfill that purpose to Your glory and to the good of those who are friends. In Your name I pray. Amen.

Designer Fear

The fear of you and the terror of you will
be on every beast of the earth and on every
bird of the sky; with everything that creeps
on the ground, and all the fish of the sea.

GENESIS 9:2

God, the thumbprint of Your design in creation can be found in the behavior of a lot of wild animals when they see me. You said they'll be afraid of me—and how true that is for most. A wild turkey sees me, gives its warning cluck, runs, and very often takes flight. A deer stomps, raises its big white tail, and takes off like a bullet. A rabbit runs into its hole, a squirrel quickly climbs a tree, a snake slithers away, a bear bounds off. I can see this distinct trait is good for their survival—and for mine. It wouldn't be safe for me if some of them had no fear when I showed up. Thank You for giving me the wisdom to know the difference between the animals that fear me and the ones that don't. You are a wise Creator indeed. Amen.

Faithful Worker

*Whatever your hand finds to
do, do it with all your might.*

ECCLESIASTES 9:10

I'm truly grateful for my job, Lord, but I can't hide the fact from You that there are days I'd rather be hunting. Sometimes the daily grind gets so tough that my very soul needs the break that being outdoors provides. I know I need to remember that being diligent to do my work and being faithful to do it as best I can doesn't go unnoticed by You. I want You to get the glory for it. And perhaps the mouths that are fed by my work will someday speak of Your goodness to others who need to hear it. What a great reward that would be. Amen.

Holy Boldness

Peter and John answered and said to them,
"Whether it is right in the sight of God to
give heed to you rather than to God, you
be the judge; for we cannot stop speaking
about what we have seen and heard."

ACTS 4:19-20

Lord Jesus, You know very well that I live in a time when there's more and more cultural pressure to be quiet about Jesus. I pray for holy boldness to respond to that pressure the way Peter and John did. In Your mighty name I pray. Amen.

We're Gonna Talk About Jesus

Peter and John were on their way up to the temple
When they prayed in Jesus' name and God healed
    a cripple
The rulers and elders didn't like what they did so
    they jailed 'em
And said, "Don't use that name around here, it's
    not welcome"
But they said…

We can't stop talking 'bout Jesus, there's just too
much to tell
He's the One who came to save us and He made
the cripple well
You can put us on trial for saying the name of the
One who died to redeem us
Do what you will, but we won't be still, we're gonna
talk about Jesus

After two thousand years it appears not that much
is different
That name of Christ still offends and many don't
want to hear it
Our makers of law want us all to be quiet
But just like Peter and John we won't be silent

No, we can't stop talking 'bout Jesus, there's just
too much to tell
He's the One who came to save us and He made
the cripple well
You can put us on trial for saying the name of the
One who died to redeem us
Do what you will, but we won't be still, we're gonna
talk about Jesus[7]

Stick and String

God has chosen the weak things of the
world to shame the things which are strong.

1 CORINTHIANS 1:27

God, when I read today's verse, I think of how that divine irony is illustrated at a deer camp during archery season. A hunter shows up with his new high-powered, heavy-punching, technically sophisticated compound bow equipped with lighted sights, noise dampeners, and other bells and whistles. With a draw weight of 75 pounds, the techno bow has tremendous power. The hunter enjoys the envious oohs and aahs as he removes it from its case. Then a guy arrives with an ancient-styled bow, which is essentially a stick and a string. The simple weapon has no fancy sights and a draw weight of an unimpressive 45 pounds. The group feels sorry for the man—until the hunt is over, and he's the only one who leaves with a trophy kill. The other hunters leave knowing it's not how powerful the machine is, but who is pulling the string.

Lord, I'm more like that stick-and-string bow. But if You're the One pulling the string, I can hit the mark and confound the strong so they'll be drawn to You. May it be so for Your glory. Amen.

God Is Watching

*My eyes are on all their ways...nor is
their iniquity concealed from My eyes.*

JEREMIAH 16:17

Father in heaven, help me always remember that no matter where I am, what I'm doing, what I'm saying, or where I'm going, Your loving eyes follow me. I know Your eyes are always on me, but it's not because You want to destroy me or make my life void of pleasure. Instead, it's because You love me. You're like a watchful game warden whose mission is to help hunters like me be safe as I enjoy the outdoors. I want to especially keep in mind that I can't hide my sin from Your eyes and yet You still care. That too is a sign of Your fathomless love. Knowing I'm being watched sure does make me think carefully about my actions. Thank You for loving me in this way. Blessed be Your name. Amen.

Pretasting My Thoughts

Let your speech always be with grace, as though seasoned with salt, so that you will know how you should respond to each person.

COLOSSIANS 4:6

L ord, I don't know who came up with the saying "Boys will be boys," but I wonder if they thought of it while sitting at a campfire with a bunch of verbally mischievous hunters. The talk can get a little crude in that setting. Paul's admonition about speech is worth remembering. We hunters understand the idea of salting meat to make it taste better. We season it until it tastes good to us, and when it does, we know it will taste good to those we give it to. When you tell us to season our words with salt, we understand why You want us to speak with grace. If our words taste good to us, we know they will taste good to those who hear them.

Help me not forget to pretaste my thoughts before I serve them as words on the platter of my tongue. I want to please You and not leave a bad taste with those who hear me. In Christ's name, amen.

Two Spellings

An excellent wife, who can find?
For her worth is far above jewels.

PROVERBS 31:10

Lord, for the married deer hunter, it's sometimes easy to forget that the word "deer" has another spelling: "d-e-a-r." When deer season comes around and the fair chase begins, the attention of the husband/hunter tends to head to the hollows. I can't hide the fact that I'm prone to get so focused on *deer* that my *dear* faces the undeserved threat of becoming a "deer widow." Jesus, forgive me for the times I've let this happen. Grant me the strength I need to avoid it in the future. You have indeed given me a tremendous gift in my wife. Her worth is far above jewels...and antlers. Amen.

Wind—Friend or Foe?

When a moderate south wind came
up...they weighed anchor and began
sailing along Crete, close inshore. But
before very long there rushed down from
the land a violent wind, called Euraquilo;
and when the ship was caught in it and
could not face the wind, we gave way
to it and let ourselves be driven along.

ACTS 27:13-15

God and Maker of all nature, I'm amazed how the wind is a friend one minute and a foe the next. It can be coming from a deer toward me, working in my favor, and suddenly shift and work against me. This exchange of advantage appears to be what happened to the passengers on the ship. The wind was favorable but then changed. However, You had a plan. The apostle Paul's wind-tossed journey included faith-building lessons for him, for everyone aboard, and eventually for me.

I pray Your grace will sail with me as I let the wind of Your will drive me along. In Christ's name, amen.

Sing a New Song

I will sing a new song to You, O God.

PSALM 144:9

Lord, I've learned by observing the habits of certain animals that it's not wise to do the exact same thing day after day. If I'm around and holding a turkey tag, a group of wild birds are making a big mistake if they enter the same stand of white pines every evening at a certain time. Allowing me to "pattern their movement" will result in one of them ending up in my skillet. The smart thing for them to do is change up the norm or, as the psalmist put it, "sing a new song." For the sake of spiritual safety, it makes sense to avoid vain repetition when I worship You. I want to keep in mind that if the devil knows my spiritual habits, he'll know where and when to pounce. However, singing a new song can be a way to throw off his schemes. For this reason, Father, teach me a new song, and I will sing it to You. Amen.

Back to the Blood

They overcame him because of the blood
of the Lamb and because of the word of
their testimony, and they did not love
their life even when faced with death.

REVELATION 12:11

Back to the Blood

As I follow You on the narrow road
Sometimes the cares of this life
Fall like a cloud around my soul
And steal Your love from my sight
But when I need my hope renewed
Faith has taught me what to do

I go back to the blood
Up to the place
There on that hilltop
Where Your red drops of grace
Fell to the ground
And gave me a sign
That I am Yours
And You are mine
I go back to the blood

Somehow the accuser
Knows when I'm weak
That's when he comes
And whispers to me
Tells me I'm hopeless
Redemption has failed
But that's when I follow
That crimson trail
I go back to the blood![8]

God Shoots Straight with Crooked Bows

[Abram] believed in the LORD; and He reckoned it to him as righteousness.

GENESIS 15:6

Father of mercy, even though Abram had some flaws, how kind You were to him to reward his belief in You by counting him as righteous. I'm grateful that this is true not only for him but also for me. Your willingness to consider my belief in You as righteousness has literally redeemed my life. You give me purpose. You're like a bow maker who looks at a crooked stave from an Osage orange tree and sees its warps, but because the wood yields to the skill of the craftsman who knows how to work with it, it is made into a weapon that can shoot true.

You did that for me, Father. Even though I'm flawed, my believing in You and yielding to You made me worthy and available to be used by You. What a great and mighty God You are to be able to shoot straight with a crooked bow like me. Amen.

Great Gain

Godliness actually is a means of great gain
when accompanied by contentment.

1 TIMOTHY 6:6

O Father in heaven, surely You know what a challenge it is these days to be content. In just the field of hunting, there's always something else to want. The companies that make outdoor gear count on my lack of contentment for their gain. The truth is, if I buy into that, even if I get the latest gadget, my happiness will last only until they release an upgraded model. I can see how that becomes my loss because discontentment is a trail that leads to more want. There's no good feeling that comes with never being satisfied. However, because the pursuit of godliness brings the truest kind of contentment, I want to feel the gain of that joy. What more could I want? I pray for Your grace to lead me on the path of righteousness. Amen.

The Sting Is Gone

The perishable must clothe itself with the imperishable, and the mortal with immortality. When the perishable has been clothed with the imperishable, and the mortal with immortality, then the saying that is written will come true: "Death has been swallowed up in victory."

1 CORINTHIANS 15:53-54 NIV

O Lord my God, how painful it is to say farewell to a fellow hunter. In times of grief, we look for comfort. We listen for words from others that will soothe, but as kind as their words are, we still struggle to find solace. Then we wisely turn to Your Word. There You remind us that when the body of our dear one perishes, in that moment his or her spirit passes through the veil of time and takes on immortality. In that instant, like a vicious scorpion that has had its stinger ripped out, death loses its hurting power and is forever harmless to the one we cared for so much. How wonderful to know that You defeated death in this way. It certainly eases the pain in times of grief. I praise You for the comfort only You can give. Amen.

Straight Arrows

*Like arrows in the hand of a warrior, so
are the children of one's youth. How
blessed is the man whose quiver is full
of them; they will not be ashamed when
they speak with their enemies in the gate.*

PSALM 127:4-5

Father in heaven, if children are like arrows in the hand of a warrior, that means eventually they'll leave the bow and fly to the place where the warrior aimed them. I pray for the parents, especially dads, that they'll be committed and determined to shape their arrows through the straightening power of Your Word and prepare them through discipline tempered by love. Compel dads and moms to aim their arrows at the target of righteousness. I also pray for all the arrows that have been set to flight. May You give them a sense of divine purpose. You know very well, God, that our nation and our world need arrows that will sail true into Your service. May it be done to Your glory. Amen.

The Hunter's Hazard

It is vain for you to rise up early,
to retire late, to eat the bread of
painful labors; for He gives to
His beloved even in his sleep.

PSALM 127:2

Lord, the psalmist says rising up early and staying up late is vanity. Whether he meant it's futile or prideful, one thing is for sure—it's a routine that can be hazardous to the health and well-being of a hunter. A long season of getting up before dawn to hunt and working until late at night can be exhausting. What's worse, I'm not the only one who suffers when I deprive myself of rest. I know the fatigue I feel is a result of my own actions, but striking a balance is a huge challenge. My request is that You will strengthen my resolve as I strive to be more sensible with my time during hunting season. I know my family, friends, and coworkers will be grateful that I came to You about this struggle. Thank You for knowing my weakness and loving me anyway. Amen.

Crying Brings Rejoicing

*The righteous cry, and the Lord hears and
delivers them out of all their troubles.*

PSALM 34:17

Lord, when I hear a fawn, a baby crow, a newborn beagle, or any other young creature crying out, what I'm hearing is the sound of life. As odd as it may sound, crying brings joy. In a hospital delivery room, the celebration begins when the mother, the doctor, and everyone in the room hears the baby cry. The noise is music to people's ears. When Your children cry, the sound is pleasing to You. It indicates the presence of life. Sadly, the opposite is also true. If there's no cry, there's probably a problem.

I pray for the courage to cry out to You, and I thank You that You hear me when I do. You are indeed a kind and loving Father. Amen.

Red Sky Predictor

*When it is evening, you say, "It will be
fair weather, for the sky is red." And
in the morning, "There will be a
storm today, for the sky is red and
threatening." Do you know how to
discern the appearance of the sky, but
cannot discern the signs of the times?*

MATTHEW 16:2-3

L ord, many times I've seen a red-sky evening and
thought, *Aha! It's going to be good weather for hun-
tin' tomorrow.* Or I see a red-sky morning and smile.
*This is good. The deer will be moving because of the
weather change.* I'm grateful for such dependable signs
You've built into nature.

I'm one of those who is better at predicting the
weather than discerning the signs of the times. What
an incredible gift to be able to see the signs of the times
that can alert us to coming events that will greatly
impact our world. I don't want to miss or ignore any
signs You send to us. Please teach me through Your
Word so I will understand what to look for and how
to prepare for whatever is ahead. In the name of the
all-seeing Savior, Christ Jesus, amen.

Seeing Their Faith

Some men were carrying on a bed
a man who was paralyzed... They
went up on the roof and let him down
through the tiles with his stretcher, into
the middle of the crowd, in front
of Jesus. Seeing their faith, He said,
"Friend, your sins are forgiven you."

LUKE 5:18-20

Lord Jesus, in the story of the paralytic You healed, I find it awe-inspiring that it was the faith of the man's friends that got Your attention. How wonderful for the paralyzed man to have people who cared that much for him. And how great that You still respond today to the faith of friends who bring buddies to You in prayer. I'm so thankful that when one of my friends is dealing with a situation that has paralyzed them emotionally and spiritually, I can bring my faith to You on their behalf and ask You to raise them up from their pallet of despair. Thank You for hearing my prayer as well as the prayers of other friends who are, by faith, carrying these needy ones into Your presence. Blessed be Your gracious, loving name. Amen.

The Dancing Leaf

Michal…saw King David
leaping and dancing before the
LORD; and she despised him.

2 SAMUEL 6:16

God, there's a happening in nature that can be quite annoying to a hunter. The air seems still, but we see movement. A single leaf in our peripheral vision responds to the barely noticeable effects of a rising thermal. As the leaf slowly sways back and forth, it repeatedly fools us into thinking an animal is moving in. After repeated adrenaline highs and letdowns, we want to shoot that leaf. The only redeemable thing about the leaping leaf is that it's a good picture of people responding to the joyous wind of Your Holy Spirit. As they display the peace and contentment You give, they catch the eyes of those nearby. Some may respond like Saul's daughter, Michal, who spurned David's joy. But when we're dancing like David, others may want to know more about where our happiness comes from and seek You. I pray for the same courage David had to respond to the joy of being Your child. I know You won't be annoyed! Amen.

Shine Through Me

Many are saying, "Who will show us any good?" Lift up the light of Your countenance upon us, O LORD!

PSALM 4:6

Father in heaven, just as it was back in Bible times, there are people today who wonder if anyone can show them anything good. David's answer is as timely now as it was when he wrote it, but it's a sobering one. When he prayed, "Lift up the light of Your countenance upon us, O LORD," he was asking You to shine through Your people so those who were looking for goodness could see You, the only One who is good. As Your follower, O Lord, I don't take that responsibility lightly. I pray Your grace will fill me so You'll be seen in my life. May it be so to Your glory and for the sake of leading others to You. In the name of Jesus I pray. Amen.

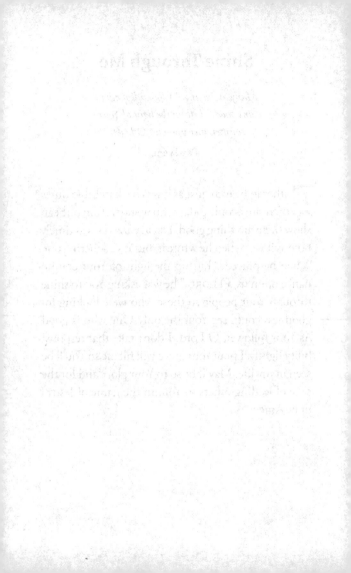

Notes

1. Steve Chapman and Jeff Pearles, "Carry Them Back," Times & Seasons Music/Jefed Music, BMI, 2014.

2. Steve Chapman, "Remember Me," Times & Seasons Music, BMI, 2013.

3. Steve Chapman, "Shell of a Man," Times & Seasons Music, BMI, CMG, 2003.

4. Steve Chapman, "Faithfully Follow You," Times & Seasons Music, BMI, 2000.

5. Steve Chapman and Dana Bacon, "Treasures," Times & Seasons Music/Dana Bacon Music, BMI, 2014.

6. Steve Chapman, "Prayer for My Child" © as "Wednesday's Prayer," Times & Seasons Music, BMI, 1996.

7. Steve Chapman, "We're Gonna Talk About Jesus," Times & Seasons Music, BMI, 2014.

8. Steve Chapman, "Back to the Blood," Times & Seasons Music, BMI, 2015.

More Great Harvest House Books
for Sportsmen *by Steve Chapman*

To learn more about Harvest House books and
to read sample chapters, visit our website:

www.harvesthousepublishers.com

HARVEST HOUSE PUBLISHERS
EUGENE, OREGON